O9-BTO-826

MYST III
EXILE

Prima's Official Strategy Guide

Rick Barba

Prima Games
A Division of Prima Communications, Inc.

3000 Lava Ridge Court
Roseville, CA 95661
(916) 787-7000
www.primagames.com

ISBN: 0-7615-3160-2
Library of Congress Catalog Card Number: 2001086278
Printed in the United States of America

01 02 03 04 BB 10 9 8 7 6 5 4 3 2 1

Acknowledgements

My first thanks go to the amazing people at Presto Studios for not only bringing everyone such a fun, fabulous game, but also for the indispensable help they provided to the writing of this book. In particular, my deepest gratitude goes to marvelous Mary DeMarle, the game's writer, and Phil Saunders, creative director, for such prompt, patient guidance despite the exigencies of their own crushing deadlines. Thanks also to Greg Uhler, producer, for his timely assistance as time got tight.

Grateful thanks go as well to the efficient, good-natured folks at Game Studios for providing the best support I've ever received from a game licensor. Special acknowledgement to Dan Irish, producer, Daniel Achterman, associate producer, and Ashley Bushore, assistant producer, for their responsiveness and attention to detail. It was truly a pleasure to work with these people.

Finally, eternal thanks go to my Prima editorial team for their usual grace under fire and stellar support. Jennifer Crotteau, David Mathews, and Terri Stewart—you are simply the best in the business.

Rick Barba
Boulder, CO
April 3, 2001

Foreword vii

Introduction viii

How to Use This Book viii
> The Golden Path Walkthrough ix
> Soft Hints ix
> Historian's Journal x
> Atrus' Journal x

Chapter 1: Tomahna 1

Sun Room 3
> Alternate Interactions 4
Atrus' Study 5

Chapter 2: J'nanin–The Lesson Age 9

Observatory: Exterior (Top Floor) 11
Island Perimeter 12
The Greenhouse 15
Observatory: Interior (First Floor) 16
The Elevator Puzzle 19
> The Lever-Weights 21
> The Crank-Wheel 21
> The Gear Switch 22
> The Rotational Gears 23
Observatory: Interior (Second Floor) 24
> Linking Book Telescopes 25
Getting From J'nanin to Voltaic: The Energy Puzzle 28
> The Light Gun 29
> The Reflection Poles 30
> The Prism and the Color Wheel 33
> The Voltaic Book Code 35
Getting From J'nanin to Amateria: The Dynamic Forces Puzzle . . 36
Getting From J'nanin to Edanna: The Nature Puzzle 39

Chapter 3: Voltaic–The Age of Energy 45

The Small Isle 47

Prima's Official Strategy Guide

Power Plant 49
   Control Tower. 50
   Gear Platform 52
   Waterwheel Corridor (Vanes) 53
Electromagnet Chamber 55
The Chasm. 60
Airship Dry Dock 61
Lava Chamber. 63
Airship Dry Dock (Valve Puzzle) 69
   Valve Tower (The Elevator). 70
   Setting the Valves 70
The Chasm Gantry 73
The Inlet Gantry & Pylons 76
Back to J'nanin 79

Chapter 4: Amateria–The Age of Dynamic Forces 82

Arrival: Pagoda Walkway 84
Balance Bridge 86
   The Lookout 87
   Control Panel 88
   Weight Room. 91
   Adjusting the Fulcrum 93
The Resonance Ring Puzzle 95
   Control Panel 95
   How the Timer Works 96
   Saavedro's Cave 98
   Setting the Resonance Rings 98
Turntable Tracks 104
   Control Panel 104
Tower Entry: The Hexagon Codes 107
   Tower Interior. 109
   Switchyard Puzzle Solution. 111
Back to J'nanin 113

Chapter 5: Edanna–The Nature Age 115

Deadwood Ridge 117
   Arrival: Middle Ridge 118
   Upper Ridge. 119

Lower Ridge: The Swing Vine 123
Edanna Forest 128
Edanna Swamp 139
   Darker Chamber 139
   Lighter Chamber 141
The Grossamery Nest 145
Back to J'nanin 146

Chapter 6: Narayan–The Age of Balance   148

Chamber Roof 150
How the Narayan Shields Work 151
Middle Floor: The Inner Shield Code 153
Bottom Floor: The Outer Shield Code 159
Endgame Scenarios 161
   Immediately Throw the Router Switch 161
   Follow Saavedro to the Glide Ship 162
   Shut Down the Power 163
   Go Back Downstairs 163
   Set Saavedro Free 164

Chapter 7: Soft Hints   165

How to Use Puzzle Hints 166
General Hints 167
Hints for J'nanin: The Lesson Age 168
   The Observatory 168
   The Energy Puzzle 170
   The Dynamic Forces Puzzle 172
   The Nature Puzzle 172
Hints for Voltaic: Age of Energy 174
   Arrival 174
   Power Plant 174
   Electromagnet Chamber 176
   Airship Dry Dock 177
   Lava Chamber 178
   The Valve Puzzle 180
   Back to J'nanin 181
Hints for Amateria: Age of Dynamic Forces 182
   Arrival 182
   Balance Bridge 182

Prima's Official Strategy Guide

Resonance Rings. 184
Turntable Tracks 185
The Central Tower. 186
Hints for Edanna: Age of Nature 188
Deadwood Ridge 188
The Bungie Swing Vine 189
Edanna Forest 190
Edanna Swamp 193
Hints for Narayan: Age of Balance 195

Chapter 8: Historian's Journal: On the Narayan Exile and the Lesson Age of Atrus   198

Atrus Creates the Lesson Age 199
Narayan's Symbiosis: Culture and Tradition. 200
Atrus and Saavedro 201
Sirrus and Achenar: Decay of Narayani Tradition. 203
Saavedro's Dilemma 204
Saavedro on J'nanin 204
A New Link to J'nanin 205
Saavedro's Scheme 206

Chapter 9: Atrus' Journal   207

Maps

Atrus' Study and Sun Room, Tomahna 2
Overhead, J'nanin 10
Overhead, Voltaic. 46
Overhead, Amateria 83
Deadwood Ridge, Edanna 116
Lower Ridge Cutaway, Edanna 123
Forest Area, Edanna 128
Swamp, Edanna 139
Middle Floor, Narayan 149
Overhead Roof, Narayan 150
Bottom Floor, Narayan. 159

Dan Irish and Daniel Achterman (Producers at Ubi Soft Entertainment)

One of the nice things about working on a project like *Myst III: Exile* is that when our friends ask us where we disappeared to for two years, we can simply hand them a box with the game in it and say "Here. Two years' worth of our creativity, hard work, and dedication are in this box. Now go play this game or you can't be our friend anymore." I'm sure the guys at Presto Studios feel the same way. Making *Myst III: Exile* into the game it is was a two-year labor of love that took everything we could give it. It is the culmination of all our previous work, and everyone who contributed to it has something to be proud of.

What amazed us more than anything through the development cycle of *Myst III: Exile* is that the game wasn't really designed, or built, so much as it was grown. It felt like a living thing sometimes. It isn't the creation of any one person, but rather the culmination of all the best ideas of a talented team. We set out to create a visually stunning and engaging interactive story that anyone anywhere can enjoy, one that stays true to the *Myst* mythology that Cyan created so long ago. Over time, ideas were added, removed, polished, and added again. It took a long time to evolve, gradually becoming more and more detailed. Puzzles were perfected and sounds were adjusted. Then one day, at last, it was finished.

It is with excited grins and great expectations that we invite you to enjoy *Myst III: Exile*. Here you go. Two years of our lives in a box. Now play it, or you can't be our friend anymore.

Presto Studios

Myst. The very name evokes a sense of intrigue, the anticipation that new discoveries will emerge from a shrouding haze. It is this sense of wonder that a talented creative team led by two brothers, Robyn and Rand Miller, managed to capture in a game that has now become a legend.

Myst created a legacy beloved of fans worldwide. It also introduced a universe as significant to interactive entertainment as *Star Wars* is to cinema and *Middle Earth* is to literature.

Imagine the honor and responsibility of being asked to create the next adventure in such a groundbreaking and cherished series. For us at Presto Studios, it has been almost overwhelming. Not simply because of what we are following, but also because of the expectation that a new *Myst* game must once again advance the art.

For the last two years we have put our art, our heart, to this goal. There has been wonder and revelation, challenge and struggle, excitement and joy in the adventure of this creation. We hope you discover the same things playing it.

Introduction

Any chronicle of the home computer's rise in the 1990s should devote an entire chapter to the *Myst* phenomenon. In 1993, the original *Myst* emerged from a Pacific Northwest garage to become the best-selling computer game of all time. Described by *The New York Times* as "a landmark in the game industry," the weirdly calm, atmospheric adventure lured millions of nongamers to previously underused monitors, injecting a healthy dose of mass-market mania into the PC industry.

And the phenomenon didn't stop with *Myst*. The game's sequel, *Riven*, became a classic in its own right (more than two million units sold to date). Then, the technically spectacular 3D recreation of the original game, *realMYST*, generated yet another stir during Christmas 2000. Now the stunning third installment, *Myst III: Exile*, is upon us.

An inspired product of the adventure game masters at Presto Studios, *Exile* adds a dramatic chapter to the saga of Atrus, writer of worlds. Each new Age features magnificent *Myst*-style scenery, fabulous creatures, the usual complement of fantastic machines and, of course, plenty of puzzles. Presto took special care to craft puzzles that flow organically from the story's environments. Of course, "organic" doesn't necessarily mean easy. In fact, many of *Exile*'s puzzles are fiendishly difficult.

And that's where we come in.

How to Use This Book

This book is designed to be easy to use. Note, however, that it is not a substitute for the *Myst III: Exile* game manual. As a "strategy guide," this book assumes you've read all of the documentation that comes with the game.

The Golden Path Walkthrough

Chapters 1 to 6 give you a detailed, step-by-step solution path through *Myst III: Exile*. The walkthrough is divided into six chapters, one for each Age you visit. Use the table of contents to find the location where you need help, then turn to the corresponding section to get all the answers you seek.

What does "golden path" mean? In this case, it means you get more than just quick, mindless solutions. You get in-depth explanations of puzzle and plot logic; you get gorgeous overhead maps of each Age, courtesy of Presto Studios; you get background information; and you get literally hundreds of helpful screenshots for visual reference. Keep in mind that it does clearly reveal complete puzzle solutions and some plot spoilers. We've included another section for those of you who want to avoid the spoilers.

Remember that although *Myst III: Exile* tells an essentially linear story, the game's 3-D world lets you, the player, "tell" that story in a variety of ways. This golden path walkthrough, based on the design team's own optimal solution path, tries to tell the story efficiently without sacrificing dramatic effect.

Soft Hints

For intrepid explorers who prefer more indirect direction, Chapter 7: Soft Hints provides tips but not answers for every major puzzle in the game. Layered carefully in lists descending from general to specific, these tips gently nudge you down the puzzle path. However, they stop just short of revealing the final solution. This section is perfect for puzzle fiends, serious self-starters, and those of us who just can't stop reading when easy answers lay at our fingertips.

Historian's Journal

Warning! Do not read Chapter 8, Historian's Journal, until you've finished the game! After you have played through to the story's end (with or without our help), take a look at this "scholarly" examination of the *Myst III: Exile* background. Developed with extensive input from *Exile*'s primary creators, Mary DeMarle (Lead Writer) and Phil Saunders (Creative Director), this section chronicles the events that lead up to your encounter with Atrus and his mysterious tormentor. In the process, it discusses many of the plot secrets revealed in the game.

Atrus' Journal

Near the beginning of the game, Atrus hands you a journal—a fascinating chronicle of his attempts to write a new Age for the D'ni. In this section, we provide the exact text of Atrus' journal as it appears in the game. Don't worry, it won't spoil anything; we just present it for your reading pleasure.

Chapter 1
Tomahna

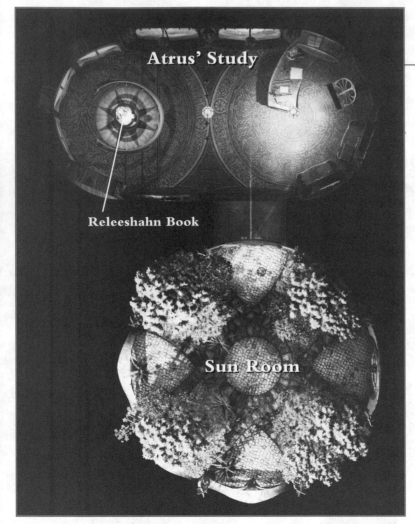

Atrus' Study

Releeshahn Book

Sun Room

Fig. 1-1. Here's an overview map of the Tomahna Sun Room and Study.

Your adventure begins in Tomahna, the high-desert home Atrus built for his family not long after the events of *Riven*—the same Tomahna mentioned in the epilogue of *Myst: The Book of D'ni* (Hyperion, 1997). The place is beautiful and serene, but recent disturbing events have put Atrus on edge.

Note: The name "Tomahna" derives from the D'ni term *eder tomahn*, which translates as a rest house or way station. In *Myst: The Book of Atrus* (Hyperion, 1995), Atrus' father Gehn leads his young son through a labyrinth of tunnels connecting underground D'ni to the surface world. Along the way, they rest in an *eder tomahn*. As Gehn explains, "In the days of the late [D'ni] empire there were plans to have commerce with the world of men. Such plans, fortunately, did not come to pass, yet the paths were forged through the earth and these rest houses prepared for the D'ni messengers who would venture out."

Sun Room

Fig. 1-2. The glass dome of Catherine's Sun Room on Tomahna.

The Sun Room is a circular chamber built into the cliffs overlooking a high-desert vista. Wrought-iron support frames sweep upward through hand-bubbled stained glass, allowing plenty of sunlight to filter in. Plants hang from the ceiling or grow in planters set into the cobblestone floor. A stone bench sits near one window. Two doors lead from the room—one into family living quarters, one into Atrus' study.

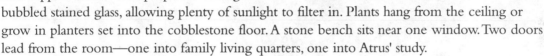

- As the game starts, you gaze out on a desert vista and hear Catherine say, "Breathtaking, isn't it?"
- Turn around to see Catherine holding her baby daughter, Yeesha.

Fig. 1-3. Meet Catherine, wife of Atrus, and their new daughter Yeesha, in the Tomahna Sun Room.

Catherine welcomes you to Tomahna, the new residence Atrus constructed after he finished "writing" the Releeshahn Age for the D'ni survivors. She apologizes for her husband's absence; he might be resetting padlocks. Apparently, Atrus has worried about security of late. However, she says, Atrus looks forward to "introducing you to the D'ni." She suggests you wait in his study, then she sits on the bench to play with Yeesha.

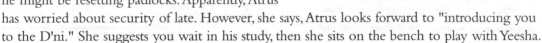

- Walk across the Sun Room toward the door straight ahead.
- Click on the door to open it.
- Enter the study.

The D'ni are an ancient race; indeed, their history stretches back many millennia. D'ni society and its majestic capital city were decimated by earthquakes and a deadly plague—a biological attack, actually—roughly 80 years prior to the events of *Myst III: Exile*.

Fig. 1-4. These tapestries in Atrus' study depict scenes of his search though the Ages for D'ni survivors.

In *The Book of D'ni*, we learn how Atrus and Catherine travel through the Ages to discover more than 1,800 D'ni survivors of the great catastrophe. At first, Atrus sought to repair the once-magnificent city. But as he reveals in *Myst III: Exile*'s opening scene, the task proved too difficult due to the depth of the tragic history contained within the city. He felt that the D'ni needed a fresh start. Thus Atrus wrote an entirely new Age for the survivors—a place he calls Releeshahn.

Alternate Interactions

- When you cross the room, your first click moves you to a position (called a "node") in the middle of the Sun Room. Here, if you swivel left to see Catherine and Yeesha on the bench, Catherine comments about Atrus' unease "ever since he found his journals out of place."

- Opposite the bench is another door. If you click on this door, you find it locked, and Catherine says, "I'm sorry, the other door."

- If you enter the study without finding Atrus, and then return to the Sun Room and look at Catherine again, she comments that her husband doesn't usually keep guests waiting, but he's "so concerned about his books."

Atrus' Study

Atrus' study is an oval chamber with opaque, circular windows. Tables and shelves filled with papers, pens, and leather-bound books line the walls. His desk sits near a set of hanging tapestries that tell the story of the D'ni survivors. On a table behind the desk sits the descriptive book for Gehn's Fifth Age. (The inscription on the cover is the D'ni numeral 5.) Also known as Riven, this legendary Age was originally written by Atrus' father, Gehn. The book's linking panel is non-functional because the unstable Age imploded. (When an Age "dies," any panels that link to it go dark.)

Fig. 1-5. The Riven descriptive book, its linking panel now darkened, sits behind Atrus' desk.

Note: For more on Gehn's Fifth Age, of course, play the Cyan classic, *Riven*. In that game, Atrus refers to "the familiar pattern of decay that is the hallmark of my father's work."

Across the room, the completed descriptive book for the Releeshahn Age, new home of the D'ni, rests on an ornate pedestal—locked shut, encased in a glass dome, and lit by a glowing D'ni fire marble.

Fig. 1-6. Examine the items on Atrus' work desk.

- Enter the room and veer to the right of Atrus' desk.

- Turn left and look down at the desktop. A handwritten letter from Atrus to "Tamon" lies there.

- Click on the letter to read it. Atrus is indeed worried about security; recently, he's suspected some trespasser has been sneaking in to read his journals.

- Examine the sketched portraits on the desk: one of Catherine and the baby Yeesha, and one of Atrus' grown sons, Sirrus and Achenar.

The letter on Atrus' desk is addressed to Tamon, an elderly D'ni guildsman who appears in *The Book of D'ni*. Tamon is a member of the D'ni Guild of Stonemasons who survived the destruction of D'ni; he was in another Age, called Aurack, at the time.

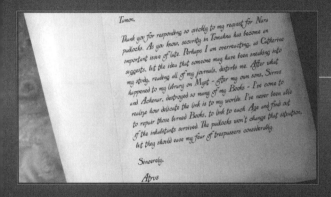

Fig. 1-7. The letter on Atrus' desk reveals his fears.

Note also the reference to *nara locks*. Nara is the hardest of all D'ni substances, "a metallic greenish-black stone thirty times the density of steel," according to *The Book of Ti'ana*. Nara is created by dumping excavated rock into a huge "fusion-compounder" machine that reconstitutes the very matter of the rock, reforging its atomic links to reduce its volume by a factor of two hundred.

Fig. 1-8. Sirrus and Achenar, of course, are the greedy, scheming brothers in the original game, Myst.

Fig. 1-9. The Releeshahn descriptive book is locked in this protective case.

🏛 Go to the Releeshahn book pedestal on the room's opposite side. Note again how the pedestal is lit by a glowing, reddish-orange orb: a D'ni fire marble.

🏛 Click on the pedestal for a close-up. The book's cover is sealed shut by an impenetrable lock.

🏛 Click again to zoom away. This triggers the entrance of Atrus, who speaks somewhere behind you. (This automatic sequence occurs only if you've already explored behind Atrus' desk. If you haven't, go there now, and then return to this spot next to the Releeshahn book.)

🏛 You automatically turn around to see Atrus approach from the study door.

Note: The remarkable D'ni fire marble is a stone that harbors great energy. When polished, it produces bright light and can be used in special lanterns. Fire marbles are combustible (a fact made plain soon by events in Atrus' office) and can be extinguished by water.

Atrus, carrying a plain-looking journal, crosses the room to greet you. He hands you the journal, explaining that it contains his commentaries on the Releeshahn Age. (The journal automatically enters your inventory.) Then Atrus goes to his desk to retrieve the key that will unlock the Releeshahn descriptive book.

Fig. 1-10. Your old friend Atrus plans to take you to Releeshahn, the new home of the D'ni people...

Fig. 1-11. ...but an intruder has other plans for the Releeshahn book.

Suddenly, a wild-looking man in ragged robes "links" into the room on the opposite side of Releeshahn's glass case. He sees you, panics, and tosses the fire marble. It explodes near the tapestries, spawning flames. Atrus reacts in horror. You hear glass break. Turning, you see the man snatch the Releeshahn Book from its now-shattered glass casing. Then he pulls out a linking book, pauses a moment, and links away.

His linking book falls to the floor.

> After the wild-looking man disappears, you see a close-up of his linking book.

> Click the book's animated panel to travel to J'nanin, the Lesson Age.

Fig. 1-12. The intruder uses this linking book, then drops it on the floor. Use it to jump to J'nanin, the Lesson Age.

Chapter 2
J'nanin
The Lesson Age

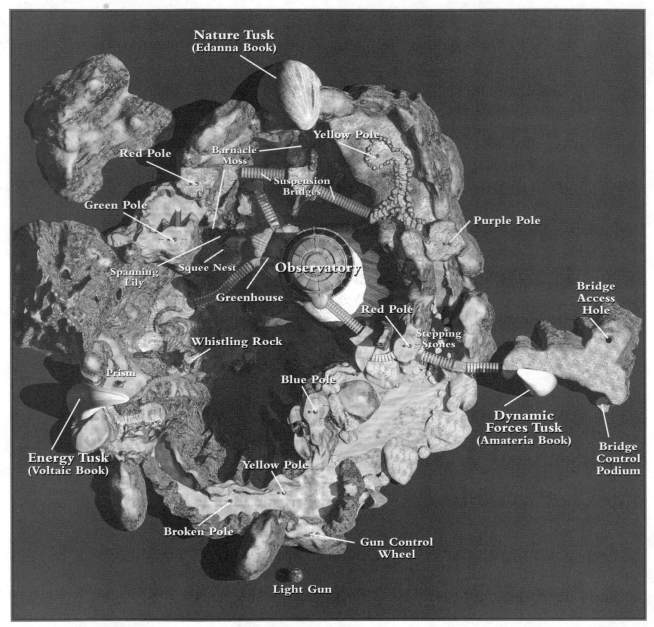

Nature Tusk
(Edanna Book)

Yellow Pole

Red Pole

Barnacle Moss

Suspension Bridges

Green Pole

Purple Pole

Spanning Lily

Squee Nest

Observatory

Red Pole

Bridge Access Hole

Greenhouse

Stepping Stones

Whistling Rock

Prism

Blue Pole

Dynamic Forces Tusk
(Amateria Book)

Bridge Control Podium

Energy Tusk
(Voltaic Book)

Yellow Pole

Broken Pole

Gun Control Wheel

Light Gun

Fig. 2-1. Overhead map of J'nanin, the Lesson Age.

Welcome to J'nanin. Formed by an extinct volcano rising from a pristine ocean, J'nanin is a stark, striking island Age. A ring of sheer cliffs encircles a fresh-water caldera lake; paths and stairs line the cliff walls, and three strange, tusk-like towers punctuate the perimeter of the island.

You arrive without a linking book, but fortunately other linking books are scattered about the island. Each links to one of the "Element Ages" which Atrus created to teach lessons associated with the ancient D'ni art of writing Ages. Your eventual goal is to find and use these books. Your immediate task, however, is to gain access to the top floor of the towering Observatory above J'nanin's central lake.

Fig. 2-2. You must get to the top floor of the Observatory.

Observatory: Exterior (Top Floor)

You arrive in J'nanin just in time to see a wild-looking man run across a short, curving catwalk and disappear behind an outcropping of rock. He carries the Releeshahn descriptive book. An odd view-scope (topped by a red fire marble) juts up from the ground nearby. This device is called a "reflection pole"—you'll learn why later. For now, follow that thief!

Fig. 2-3. Note the "reflection pole" with the red fire marble on top—one of many such poles on the island.

- Cross the short catwalk to see the man reach the top of a ladder and disappear again.

- Approach the ladder.

- Click on the ladder to climb the cliff. At the top, you see the man open the Observatory door, then shut it behind him.

The two-story Observatory is the most prominent man-made structure on the island. Its second floor juts above the caldera's cliffs; its first floor nestles inside the crater's basin.

Fig. 2-4. The thief paces in the Observatory's inner chamber.

- Cross the high bridge and try to open the door. It's locked!

- Click on the door's window. You see the wild-haired fellow pacing in a chamber beyond a second, inner door.

Island Perimeter

Well, now what?

There must be another way into this huge structure. Perhaps an examination of the tower's base is in order. But first, spend some time with the journal Atrus handed you before the stranger's rude appearance back in Tomahna. Note his comments about essential concepts or "anchors" for Ages. In particular he speaks of Energy, Nature, Dynamic Forces, and Balance. Then he suggests he could relearn these concepts from "one of my oldest Age Books"—J'nanin, the very place where you stand now.

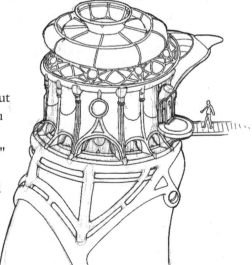

Fig. 2-5. First things first. Read the journal Atrus gave you to learn what's at stake.

In the 93.5.25 entry of Atrus' journal, he mentions "devastating events of recent months—the war on Terahnee, and the death of Uta, in particular." Terahnee is an ancient Age Atrus discovered while attempting to rebuild D'ni; its travails are chronicled in *Myst: The Book of D'ni*, (Hyperion, 1997). (See the end of this book for Atrus' complete journal.)

Closely related to the D'ni race, Terahnee followed the cruel path of Gehn, Atrus' father, by enslaving entire Ages. Eventually, a plague decimated Terahnee. The weakness of the masters prompted a bloody slave revolt. Uta was a young slave boy who died at the hands of a corrupt leader of the great Terahnee slave rebellion.

Atrus also mentions Oma and Esel in journal entry 93.10.24. These brothers are sons of one of the D'ni survivors and are self-taught historians with much knowledge of the language and culture of the D'ni. Oma and Esel became staunch allies of Atrus, joining in his efforts to restore the D'ni civilization.

- From the top of the Observatory, cross the high bridge and climb down the ladder.

- Step onto the curving catwalk, turn right, and descend the set of rungs leading down to the beach. Lovely, isn't it?

Fig. 2-6. These rungs embedded in the rock provide access to the sandy beach path.

- At the ocean, turn right. Follow the sandy path past another reflection pole, this one topped by a yellow fire marble.

- Continue past a broken reflection pole toward the tall, tusk-shaped tower.

Fig. 2-7. This broken pole marks the path to the stairway running down into the caldera.

- Turn right at the boulder that blocks your forward path and descend the first set of steps.

- Turn right and continue down the next set of steps.

You end up atop a curving metal stairway that slaloms right through the middle of a rock formation, threading it like the eye of a needle. (We'll call it the Whistling Rock.) Wind rushes through the Whistling Rock, moaning with a very distinct sound. Remember the whistling sound. You'll be encountering it in another fashion later.

Fig. 2-8. Descend the curving stairway through the Whistling Rock and listen to the wind moan.

- Descend the curving metal stairs to the next landing, then go down the last set of rock steps to the catwalk.

- Cross the catwalk, which is fabulously edged with fire marbles, to the greenhouse.

The Greenhouse

Attached to the Observatory's base is a stunning, stained-glass greenhouse. Two catwalks extend across the lake's surface, each to a separate greenhouse entrance.

Fig. 2-9. The Observatory greenhouse provides entrance into the Observatory

Fig. 2-10. Pull this release lever to open the greenhouse gate.

- Click on the door to open it, then step forward into the entryway.
- Click on the lever to pull it down, activating a gate release mechanism.

Fig. 2-11. Press this button to open the inner gate to the Observatory's first floor.

- Go through the gate and push the button on the right. The gate behind you opens.

- Enter the Observatory.

Observatory: Interior (First Floor)

The Observatory's first floor is a circular chamber with a high ceiling. Lately, somebody has made this area his home; you find a sleeping hammock and a journal. You also discover some interesting devices scattered about the room, a work desk, and an elevator car in an ornate metal cage.

- From the doorway, swivel to the right and approach the hammock.

- Click on the leather journal to take it from the hammock.

- Open the journal and read all entries. Among other bits of information, it contains the key for realigning the elevator's rotational gears.

Fig. 2-12. Don't miss this journal lying on the hammock.

The journal tells you a great deal about the mysterious wild-haired thief, including his name, Saavedro, and his motivation, revenge. Clearly, he's found a link to Tomahna, and has become familiar with Atrus' journals. Saavedro's hatred for Atrus and his "murdering sons" (Sirrus and Achenar) is deep and burning, based on a belief that they betrayed his home Age of Narayan and, as he writes, "led my people to death."

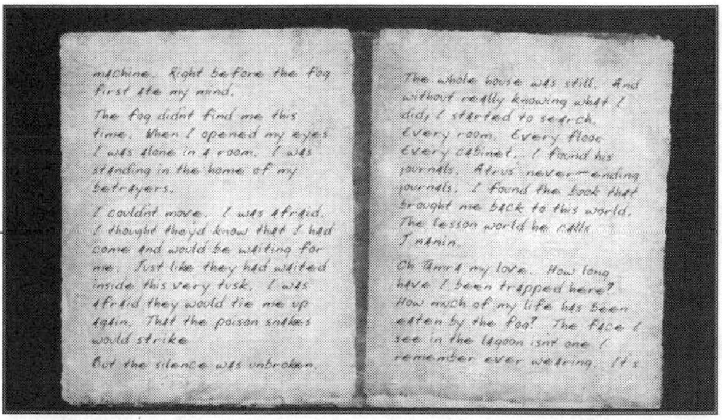

Fig. 2-13. Saavedro's journal reveals his motivations, as well as some important sketches for the elevator mechanism.

You also learn that the Age you currently inhabit is called J'nanin, "The Lesson Age." Note that Saavedro has linked to other Ages where he's made alterations, "using his [Atrus'] own lessons against him." His journal also makes clear another sad fact: Saavedro mistakenly believes that Atrus' efforts to give his D'ni brethren "new life"—that is, a new Age, Releeshahn—means Atrus has somehow resurrected the perished D'ni civilization. Saavedro writes: "How can one man's writings reawaken a dead world?"

Thus, his goal: Lure Atrus from Tomahna to J'nanin, then seek the restoration of Narayan—or, failing that, vengeance.

Note: Close perusal of Saavedro's journal reveals that many pages are missing. Being Narayan, he numbered the pages using the Narayan numbering system. That system is pictorial; as with most things in the Narayan culture, it is tied to the concept of the Lattice Tree. A single vertical line represents the number 1: the tree trunk. Every time you add a number, you add a branch to the tree.

So the Narayan numeral 2 is the trunk with one branch. The number 3 is the trunk with two branches forming a Y. For 4, one of the branches in the Y sprouts an additional branch pointing back toward the trunk, and 5 adds the inward growing branch on the opposite side of the tree.

For 6 through 9, you start with the character for 5 and draw a new trunk next to it. (Think Roman numerals: Just as VI is the Roman 6, the Narayan 6 looks like a 5 with a 1 next to it, 7 looks like a 5 with a 2 next to it, and so on.) Once you get to 10, things change a little. The Narayan 10 is a 5 with a semicircle topping it. But then we go back to Roman numeral styling: 11 is a 10 with a 1 next to it, 15 is a 10 with a 5 next to it, and 16 is a 10 with a 5 and a 1 next to it.

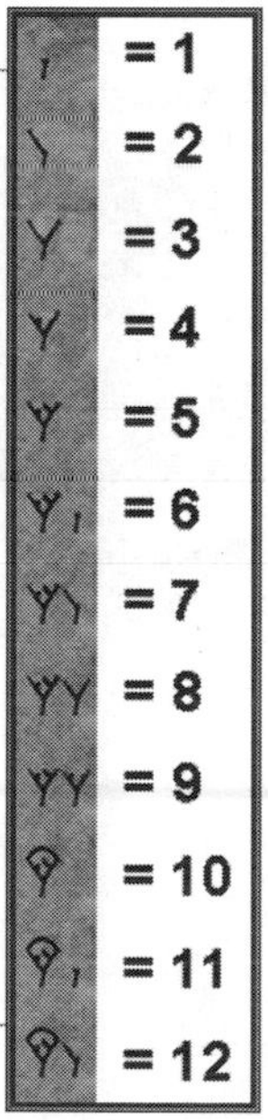

	= 1
	= 2
	= 3
	= 4
	= 5
	= 6
	= 7
	= 8
	= 9
	= 10
	= 11
	= 12

Fig. 2-14. Who is this woman on the wall? An image of Tamra, the lost love spoken of in Saavedro's journal? Why are her eyes missing?

🐚 Approach the Observatory workbench and experiment with Saavedro's devices to find out what they do.

🐚 A crank-powered battery sits between a conch-shaped terrarium (left) and an electromagnetic device (right). Wires run from the battery's terminals to the electromagnetic device.

🐚 Turn the battery crank. This sends power to the device's magnet, levitating a handful of metal shavings inside the device.

Fig. 2-15. Examine the odd devices on Saavedro's workbench. This battery powers two very different items.

🐚 A strange plant resembling a Venus flytrap grows in the terrarium. One of its roots extends across the table near the battery wires. Click on the battery wires to detach them from the device wires and attach them to the plant root.

🐚 Turn the battery crank again. The power surge causes the plant to open up briefly, release a fly and reveal the plant's inner cavity. After a moment, the plant clamps shut on the unfortunate insect.

🐚 Now examine the other interactive objects in the room.

🐚 Two balances with equal-sized weights made of three different materials (metal, crystal, and wood) sit in the room: one on the work desk, and the other next to the hammock. Examine these devices to discover how many weights of one material equal how many weights of the others—a crucial clue to solving a later puzzle.

Fig. 2-16. These two scales indicate that the weight of one metal sphere equals four crystal spheres, and one crystal sphere equals four wooden spheres.

- A miniature fulcrum toy, with two fixed weights attached to one end and exactly half that amount attached to the other, sits on the other side of the hammock. (That wouldn't be Atrus & Sons hanging in effigy, would it?) Examine it to discover how to achieve balance despite the uneven distribution of weight. Why? We're not telling yet.

- Approach the elevator.

The Elevator Puzzle

The elevator is a sleek wooden car surrounded by a metal cage. This cage has a series of retractable claws that can lock onto the wooden car. A nearby lever rotates the cage 180 degrees; if the cage claws are locked, the wooden car rotates too. This car rotation is important because it lines up the elevator's door with the inner door on the Observatory's upper level. If you don't rotate the elevator car, you can't get into the upstairs chamber.

Fig. 2-17. This elevator provides access to the Observatory's top level, but only if rotated properly.

Of course, Saavedro (as mentioned in his journal) has scavenged parts from the cage mechanism; as a result, the claws don't automatically lock onto the wooden car. If the claws don't lock, only the outer cage rotates. But Saavedro writes that "the gears I leave can still be operated by hand." These gears are in a crawl space below the elevator.

- Walk around the elevator and click on the handles on the wall, for a close-up view.
- Pull the handles to send the elevator car up, revealing a small crawl space at the bottom of the shaft.
- Back away from the close-up, and then go down into the crawl space.
- Examine the crawl space. Four compartments arrayed around the shaft have been forcibly breached, revealing various gears and mechanisms.
- Open Saavedro's journal and examine his sketches of the elevator gears and mechanisms.
- Pick up the journal and keep it with you.

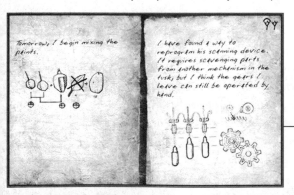

Fig. 2-18. These sketches from Saavedro's journal show the settings for the four mechanisms in the elevator crawl space.

Saavedro's journal reveals the gear settings necessary to re-activate the cage claws and thus rotate the elevator car. You must adjust all four gear-driven mechanisms. Refer to figure 2-18 to see Saavedro's sketches of the four settings, or just check out figures 2-19 through 2-22 to see the actual settings.

The Lever-Weights

The first mechanism is a set of three lever-weights. Each weight can be manipulated up/down to one of three positions: top, middle, bottom. To correctly adjust the lever-weight settings:

- Click the leftmost lever-weight twice. This drops the weight to its bottom setting.

- Don't adjust the center lever-weight. This leaves the weight at its middle setting.

- Click the rightmost lever-weight twice. This raises the weight to its top setting, then lowers it to its middle setting.

- Now all three lever-weights are in the correct positions (as seen in figure 2-19). From left, settings are bottom, middle, middle.

Fig. 2-19. Final settings for the lever-weights.

The Crank-Wheel

After you adjust the lever-weights, swivel to the next compartment to the right. Through the breach you can see one arm of a three-armed crank-wheel. Each arm has an adjustable bolt at its tip. You can flip each bolt 180 degrees, thus alternating it between two positions.

- Examine the first arm visible through the breach. See the bolt at the end of the arm? One end of the bolt is smooth; the other end is threaded.

- Move the Pointer cursor over the bolt. Click to flip the bolt 180 degrees. The threaded end should be exposed now, pointing left.

Fig. 2-20. Flip the first two end-bolts so their threaded ends face left. Leave the third unflipped and visible through the hole.

- Move the cursor up until it becomes the Open Hand cursor, then click on the wheel to rotate the second arm into view.

- Again, move the Pointer cursor over the end bolt. Click to flip the bolt. As on the previous arm, the threaded end should be exposed, pointing left.

- Don't adjust the bolt on this arm! Leave it as is. The crank-wheel mechanism is now properly set.

The Gear Switch

After you adjust the crank–wheel, swivel to the next compartment to the right. Through the breach you can see a switch that toggles a metal rod between a small gear and a large gear. (Only a few teeth of the large gear are visible in the opening.) In its present setting, the switch is pushed away from you, locking the rod into the teeth of the small gear.

Fig. 2-21. Simply click the gear switch to pull the rod toward you.

- Move the cursor over the mechanism until it becomes the Open Hand cursor.

- Click once to pull the switch towards you. The metal rod locks into the teeth of the large gear.

- Done! The gear switch is now set properly.

The Rotational Gears

After you adjust the gear switch, swivel right toward the final open compartment. Through the breach you can see a pair of meshed gears. The upper gear features a gap where a gear tooth would be normally.

Fig. 2-22. Line up the gap on the upper gear with a tooth on the lower gear.

- Move the cursor over the upper gear until it becomes the Open Hand cursor.
- Click and hold to rotate the upper gear. Keep rotating until the gap in the upper gear aligns with a tooth of the lower gear (as seen in figure 2-22).

All four mechanisms are now set so that the cage claws will lock onto the elevator and rotate the car. Let's take a trip upstairs, shall we?

- Climb out of the crawlspace.
- Click on the wall handles again for a close-up.
- Pull the handles to bring the elevator car down.
- Open the car door and step inside the elevator.
- Turn to find the handles, accessible through an opening in the elevator's wall.
- Pull the handles.

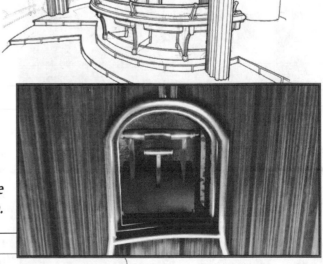

Fig. 2-23. Inside the elevator, pull down the handles to activate the rotational mechanism.

Note: You must have the Journal for the elevator to function correctly.

Again, the handles activate the cage. If you set the gears properly, the cage claws lock onto the wooden elevator car and rotate it 180 degrees. The elevator then carries you up to the second level of the Observatory. At this time, a cutscene will play showing Saavedro placing a crumpled piece of paper down on the light table. This action causes a cage to rise out of the center of the room. You arrive with the door facing inward, toward the chamber.

> **Note:** If you ride the elevator to the second floor without realigning the gears first, the cage claws won't rotate the car. Thus, when you arrive upstairs, the elevator door faces the Observatory's *outer* door, and you automatically turn to see Saavedro through the elevator window. (He thinks you're Atrus.) To ride the elevator back down to the first floor, press the green button in the wall opening.

Observatory: Interior (Second Floor)

The Observatory's second floor is a large circular room with a deep, bowl-shaped pit sunk into the center. An egg-shaped cage sits atop a podium in the pit. Inside the cage rests another linking book.

Fig. 2-24. Too late! Saavedro links away, and the book sinks into the pit, out of reach.

- Open the elevator door to see Saavedro link away. After he disappears, the cage slams shut around the linking book and spins down into the pit.
- Open the inner door and step out of the elevator into the second floor chamber.
- Veer left to the opening in the railing around the center pit.
- Press the large blue button on the right side of the opening.

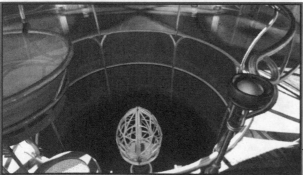

Fig. 2-25. Push the blue button at right to trigger the hologram projectors.

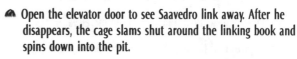
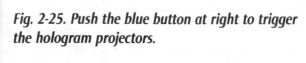

Fig. 2-26. Atrus wrote this Age to teach his sons the fundamental concepts of writing Ages. Now Saavedro wants Atrus to take his own Lesson Age course—slightly altered.

Three projectors activate, casting a three-dimensional hologram image of Atrus on the ceiling. Calling you "my sons" (referring, obviously, to Sirrus and Achenar) he speaks of three linking books on this island, each connecting to an Age. But in the midst of his instructions a second message cuts in, this one recorded by Saavedro. Calling you Atrus, he declares he's been "trapped in these Lesson Ages by two very greedy little boys"—yes, Sirrus and Achenar.

Saavedro explains he has the Releeshahn book, and if Atrus wants to reclaim it, he must follow using the caged book below. But Saavedro has changed the three symbols that unlock the cage device holding the linking book. If you hope to regain Atrus's book, you'll have to take his Lesson Ages course and discover exactly what alterations Saavedro made on each Age.

Linking Book Telescopes

Atrus installed three view-stations 120 degrees apart in the room's circular wall. Their protective shields slide open when you activate the hologram message from Atrus/Saavedro. Each station holds a telescope; each telescope allows you to view one of the three tusk-shaped towers on the island. When lined up properly, each telescope displays a "code" used later to unlock the linking book stored in the viewed tusk.

This code is visual. As you adjust the focus, zoom, and angle of each telescope's view, four metal marbles move around concentric, grooved rings surrounding the lens. The final position of these marbles is a code you must recreate later, on the podium inside the corresponding tusk (the one viewed by that telescope).

Fig. 2-27. Pan to position the tusk's symbol behind the one etched on the lens. Then use focus and zoom controls to align the two symbols (tusk and lens) precisely.

- Approach any telescope and click on it for a close-up. You see a symbol etched on the glass of the lens. Beyond that, through the lens itself, you see a partial view of the island.

- Move the cursor over the telescope lens. Then click and drag to pan the telescope's view. A tusk seems to be the most prominent landmark in sight.

- Alternately adjust the zoom and focus of each telescope to get a clear, close-up view of the tusk. How? Check out the next two steps.

- Click and drag the right handle side to side. As the handle moves, two things happen: the telescope image zooms in and out, and a small metal marble on one of the rings surrounding the lens circumnavigates its ring.

- Click and drag the left handle up or down. Again, two things happen: the image becomes more or less in focus, and the metal marble on another ring moves around the lens.

- Once you've got a close, clear view of the tusk, you should see that a symbol appears inside the tusk's window. It matches the one etched in the telescope lens! This symbol represents the Age associated with the tusk you are seeing: Voltaic, Amateria, or Edanna.

- Move the cursor over the lens once more. Then click and drag to pan the telescope's view until you have lined up precisely the tusk symbol with the lens symbol. This adjustment also slides the two remaining marbles into new positions on their rings.

- You may need to zoom in on the symbol and adjust focus again to get the two symbols (lens and tusk) matched up exactly. But when they do, the final position of all four metal marbles on their respective rings reveals the "code" needed to access the linking book inside the tusk.

Fig. 2-28. After you align each lens symbol with its corresponding tusk symbol, note the final array of the marbles around its lens. Here are the three final codes.

🐚 When moving from station to station, watch the floor. Saavedro dropped a very bitter excerpt from his journal for Atrus to find.

🐚 Pull the handle next to the exit door. This lowers the elevator so you can exit to the high bridge.

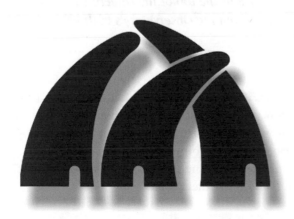

Fig. 2-29. Pull the wall handle (shown here to the right of the door) to give yourself a quick exit route.

- Open the inner door and approach the outer door.
- Click on the handle to the left of the outer door to unlock the outer door.

- Open the door and step outside onto the high bridge. Time to solve the Voltaic linking book puzzle.

Getting from J'nanin to Voltaic: The Energy Puzzle

The Voltaic linking book is located behind a locked door in the tusk-shaped tower seen in figure 2-30. Five small buttons, arrayed in a circle around the door's knob, form a combination lock. When you first see these buttons, however, you have no idea how they work.

Fig. 2-30. The Voltaic linking book chamber is in that tusk at the top of the caldera staircase. (This view is from the Observatory's high bridge.)

A small prism sits on a stand a few feet in front of the chamber door. When light shines through this prism, a color wheel is superimposed on top of the buttons. This provides the interface by which you can solve the energy puzzle, provided you've discovered the color code. To get light to shine through the prism, you must find the island's "light gun" and understand the reflection pole system.

The Light Gun

The J'nanin light gun captures light through an intake lens and redirects it through a high-powered focusing lens. The gun sits on a small outcropping of rock several feet offshore. The gun controls and the focusing lens are located nearby on the island cliffs.

- From the top of the Observatory, cross the bridge and go down the ladder.

- Step onto the curving catwalk, turn right, and climb down the rungs to the beach.

- Turn right and follow the sandy path until you reach the yellow reflection pole.

- Swivel left to see two devices on a rock overlooking the ocean. (See figure 2-31.) Approach the devices.

- Note a third device just offshore: the light gun.

Fig. 2-31. The light gun's control wheel and focusing lens overlook the ocean.

Fig. 2-32. Rotate the light gun to this position so it captures sunlight and shoots a light beam at the focusing lens.

The control wheel at right rotates the light gun. The device at left is the focusing lens. Your task is to rotate the gun until it captures sunlight and directs it into the focusing lens.

- Using the control wheel, rotate the light gun's intake lens until it lines up with a hot spot on top of the gun's metallic dome. Immediately, a beam of light flashes toward the focusing lens, which in turn shoots light at the nearby yellow reflection pole.

- Follow the light beam to the nearby yellow reflection pole.

The Reflection Poles

Reflection poles, marked at the top by different colored fire marbles, are scattered all over the island. Each contains three telescopes installed at eye level on a swiveling shaft. They can be rotated in three 120-degree increments. If you rotate the poles properly, you can send the light beam originating from the light gun on a path from pole to pole toward the prism at the Voltaic linking book chamber.

Note: Atrus designed this puzzle to be much easier than the way it is currently arrayed. The broken reflection pole complicates things considerably... as, of course, Saavedro intended.

Fig. 2-33. The light hits this first reflection pole, which is yellow. Rotate it once to redirect light toward the nearby blue pole (seen here through the yellow pole's view-scope).

- At the first reflection pole, note the color of the fire marble at its top: yellow. Keep track of the order of fire marble colors as you direct the light from pole to pole.

- Look into the view-scope where the light enters. (It faces the light gun controls.) The view centers on the broken pole just up the path, the work of Saavedro. Not good!

- Rotate the reflection pole one time. This redirects the light beam to the blue reflection pole off to your right. (If you look into the view-scope receiving light, you see the blue pole.)

- Move two clicks down the sandy path (back the way you came) and turn left to see rungs running up the rock.

- Climb the rungs to the blue reflection pole.

Fig. 2-34. Climb these rungs from the beach to the blue reflection pole.

- Rotate the blue pole once to direct the light beam to the green reflection pole across the caldera to the left. (Check the view-scope receiving light to verify that the green pole is your target.)

- Climb down to the sandy path, turn left, and work your way around the perimeter of the island: across the stepping-stones, up the rock ramp, past the purple reflection pole, and down the stone steps to a pair of suspension bridges.

- Cross *both* suspension bridges. On the far side, climb the rock steps.

Fig. 2-35. Cross both suspension bridges to reach the green reflection pole.

- At the top of the steps, climb the metal steps at left to the green reflection pole.

- Rotate the green reflection pole once to direct the light beam to the nearby red reflection pole (on the rock platform just across from you. See figure 2-36).

- Go down the metal steps and up the rock steps to the red reflection pole.

Fig. 2-36. When rotated once, the green pole (at left) directs light to the red pole seen on the nearby rock platform (at right).

- Rotate the red pole *twice* to direct the light beam to another yellow reflection pole across the caldera. (Again, you can check the target by looking through the view-scope that is receiving light.)

- Descend the rock steps, go back across the two suspension bridges, and climb the rock steps to the fork (just one click upward) in the stairway.

- Take the left fork and climb to the yellow reflection pole. (Again, this is the *second* yellow pole. You rotated another yellow pole earlier.)

- Turn this yellow reflection pole *twice* to send the beam to the nearby purple reflection pole.

- Descend the steps to the fork, veer left to take the other upward fork, and climb to the purple reflection pole.

- Turn the purple reflection pole one time. This sends the light beam at another red reflection pole—the one where you first linked into J'nanin.

Fig. 2-37. The red pole (second of its color in the series) sits atop the rock platform where you first arrived in J'nanin.

- Descend the rock ramp, cross the water under the cable-bridge using the stepping-stones, turn right, and climb up the rungs. At the top, turn right and approach the red reflection pole.

- Rotate the red reflection pole once.

- Veer to the left side of the pole and look through the scope on that side (the one receiving light). The light beam now hits a prism in front of the tusk-shaped tower on the opposite side of the caldera. Let's check it out.

Fig. 2-38. Turn the final red pole once to direct the beam to the prism (as seen here through the view-scope).

The Prism and the Color Wheel

When the light beam is channeled successfully through all seven reflection poles, the prism splits the beam into a circular spectrum, a "color wheel" pattern, superimposed over the buttons on the chamber door. Now you must figure out the correct order to push the buttons. Big hint: The path the light takes as it passes through the poles reveals a color-coded sequence—the order of fire marble colors on the poles.

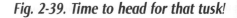

Fig. 2-39. Time to head for that tusk!

- From the final red reflection pole, step onto the curving bridge, turn left, and climb down the rungs to the beach.

- Turn right and follow the sandy path all the way up to the tusk-shaped tower.

- At the boulder that blocks your forward path, turn right and descend the first set of steps. Then turn left and climb up to the prism device in front of the structure.

Again, the light passing through the prism splits into a circular spectrum of color light waves projected onto the door. Each wave falls over a specific button, giving the button a color. The door is sealed shut by a color-coded combination lock.

Fig. 2-40. The prism splits the light beam into a color spectrum that falls over five buttons on the book chamber door.

- Enter the color code revealed by the path the light takes.

- Be more specific, you say? OK, push the door buttons in the order that matches the color sequence of the reflection pole fire marbles as you followed the light beam from the light gun through the poles to the prism. (Whew!)

- Still need help? Just push the buttons in this order: yellow, blue, green, red, yellow, purple, red. When you press the last button, the door slides open.

Note: The light beam must shine on the door before it will open. The buttons are photosensitive.

The Voltaic Book Code

You reached the linking book at last. But now what? It sits out of reach in a cage near the ceiling.

Fig. 2-41. The book is contained in a cage suspended high above your head.

- 🐚 Approach the podium beneath the cage.

- 🐚 Click on the podium for a close-up. Note the four movable marbles arrayed in concentric circular grooves. Look familiar?

- 🐚 Click and drag the marbles to the positions revealed earlier at the Observatory telescope when you focused on the Voltaic chamber (see figure. 2-42). The cage lowers.

Fig. 2-42. Move the marbles in the Voltaic podium's code-wheel to this configuration.

- 🐚 Open the Voltaic book.

- 🐚 Touch the animated panel to link to the Voltaic Age.

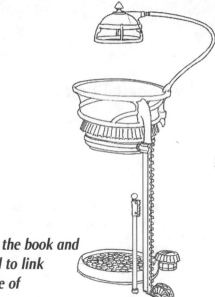

Fig. 2-43. Open the book and touch the panel to link to the Small Isle of the Voltaic Age.

Getting from J'nanin to Amateria: The Dynamic Forces Puzzle

The Amateria linking book rests in a chamber inside the tusk–shaped tower that rises from the small islet adjacent to the main landmass, near your arrival point. A large obstacle blocks your route to the book; this is the access puzzle Atrus created as the first part of his "dynamic forces" lesson plan. Unfortunately, Saavedro meddled with the plan a bit, making access to the book chamber more difficult.

Fig. 2-44. The Amateria book chamber is in this tusk rising from the small islet.

- From the top of the Observatory, cross the high bridge, climb down the ladder, and walk across the curved catwalk.

- Continue past the red reflection pole across the cable-bridge towards the tusk tower.

- Walk past the tower and veer right, moving as far forward and to the right as you can. Then look down to see the ladder rungs on the rock.

- Descend the rungs to find a podium with two levers.

Fig. 2-45. Descend these rungs to the podium.

Across a small inlet you see a large round weight on a jointed bridge. At the left end of the bridge, a door leads to the Amateria book chamber. At the right end, a bridge ladder extends to an access hole above. The weight blocks the path across the bridge. Your task here is to create an unblocked path from bridge ladder to chamber door.

- Note the four movable "bridge joints" connected to grooves in the islet's cliff. You can raise or lower these joints in inverse pairs, creating different elevation states. By manipulating these states, you can roll the round weight "downhill" along the bridge.

- Note also that the bridge ladder at right is actually attached to the bridge segment itself. Thus, it tilts away from the access hole in certain configurations; in others, it drops too low to reach the hole.

- Click the podium levers in this order: left, right, left, right. This moves the weight to the far right, unblocking the path from ladder to the tower door, and also tilts the bridge ladder back into position under the access hole.

Fig. 2-46. Move the left lever up, the right lever down, the left back down, then the right back up. This sequence rolls the weight to the far right (as seen here) and properly positions the bridge ladder.

- Ascend the rungs on the wall.

- Walk straight across the small islet to the hole. (See figure 2-47.)

- Descend the bridge ladder under the access hole and go to the tower door.

- Click on the handle to open the door. Uh oh!

Fig. 2-47. After you move the weight to the far right, descend the bridge ladder in this hole.

Look, there's the Amateria linking book—up high, locked in its cage, with the podium mechanism below. But Saavedro has somehow smashed the chamber floor: there's a wide rift between the door and the mechanism. You can't cross it. Wait… that hole looks to be roughly the size of the large weight sitting on the bridge, doesn't it?

- Return to the podium with the bridge controls.

- Roll the round weight into the tower by clicking the levers in this order: left, left, right. This rolls the weight through the open door.

- Important: Click on the right lever one more time! This tilts the bridge ladder back into position under the access hole.

- Return to the book chamber. The weight has fallen into the rift, forming a convenient "bridge" to the podium.

Fig. 2-48. Roll the weight into the book chamber to fill the floor hole, letting you cross to the podium.

- Approach the podium and click on it for a close-up.

- Click and drag the marbles to the positions revealed earlier at the Observatory telescope when you focused on the Amateria chamber (see figure 2-49). The cage lowers.

Fig. 2-49. Move the marbles in the Amateria podium's code-wheel to this configuration.

- Open the Amateria book.

- Touch the linking book panel to link to Amateria, the Dynamic Forces Age.

Fig. 2-50. Use the Amateria book to link to the Age.

Getting from J'nanin to Edanna: The Nature Puzzle

Atrus built his Edanna linking book chamber into the tusk-shaped tower nearest the Observatory. The chamber door is halfway up the tower, seemingly unreachable. But of course there is a way. And remember, Edanna is the Nature Age, so any puzzle solution in Atrus's Lesson Age will reflect that fact.

Fig. 2-51. The Edanna book chamber is halfway up this tusk. Note the melon-like buds of the Barnacle Moss on the right cliff wall.

- From the top of the Observatory, cross the high bridge, go down the ladder, and descend the rungs to the beach.

- Turn left and cross the stepping-stones under the cable-bridge. (See figure 2-52.)

Fig. 2-52. Look like a dead end? It's not. Follow those stepping-stones across the water and under the bridge.

- Walk across the stepping-stones under the cable-bridge.

- Climb the steep rock ramp on the other side. At the top, you find another reflection pole, this one with a purple fire marble.

- Turn left and descend the rock steps. At the intersection (where another set of stairs leads upward), take the left fork that leads down to a pair of suspension bridges.

- Walk across the first suspension bridge to the rock platform.

- Turn right and take a step toward the tusk-shaped tower. The linking book chamber is behind that door directly across from you.

- Look down to find the ladder, and then descend to the first landing.

Fig. 2-53. A pair of suspension bridges spans the caldera. Cross only the first bridge...

...then look down to find the rungs of a ladder.

Now take a look around. The cliff is covered with a thick green moss sprouting large, round, reddish-brown buds that look like watermelons. This is Barnacle Moss. Also note the strange plant with the ear-shaped stalk on the ledge nearby. This is a Hearken Fern. The "ear" stalk can pick up and amplify noises from distant locations if you aim it toward the sound. You'll use this plant's unique ability in a moment.

Fig. 2-54. This is a Hearken Fern. Stand behind it and give it a spin, pointing the stamen at sounds around the caldera.

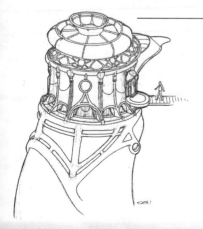

- For fun, stand behind the Hearken Fern.

- Move it around, aiming the tip of the stamen (the horn-like protrusion) at various locations across the caldera.

- In particular, aim at the lake below, the Whistling Rock formation just above it (hear the moaning?), the clouds above the caldera, and the suspension bridge just above you.

- Step past the Hearken Fern and descend the ladder down to the caldera basin.

- Move four times over the stones to the right of the catwalk. You end up next to a small tent-like structure. This is a Squee's nest.

- Push the button-like plant on the nest's top to see the Squee pop out for a look. Cute little guy, isn't he?

Fig. 2-55. Say hello to Mr. Squee. He can help you get to the Edanna book.

Time for more observation. Swivel right. See the lily-like plant in the water? That's a Spanning Lily. This flora flattens when touched and extends its spiky leaves outward. This action forms a convenient bridge for small animals to walk across water.

See the Barnacle Moss growing on the rocks across the pool? The Squee in the nest would love to feed on its delicate inner flowers. But the Squee is a land-based creature. How can it get across the water?

Fig. 2-56. When you touch the Spanning Lily, it flattens. Then call out the Squee to munch his favorite food, the Barnacle Moss.

- Touch the Spanning Lily. It retracts, spreading its leaves across the water.

- Press the top of the Squee's nest. The creature runs across to the Barnacle Moss and chirps. The sound causes the moss buds to expand. Cool!

- Retrace your steps up the ladder to the landing.

- Get behind the Hearken Fern again and point the stamen at the spot below where the Squee chirps happily. (See figure 2-57.) Wow! The amplified Squee chirping triggers the expansion of the mature Barnacle Moss buds on the cliff wall above you.

- Now climb to the top of the ladder and cross the Barnacle Moss bridge to the door in the tower.

Fig. 2-57. After you get the Squee to chirp, aim the Hearken Fern at the critter's cute sound (as shown here).

Fig. 2-58. Climb the ladder and cross those burgeoning Barnacle Moss buds to the Edanna book chamber.

- Open the door and step into the chamber. A linking book sits in a cage suspended near the ceiling, out of reach.

- Approach the podium and click on it for a close-up.

- Click and drag the marbles to the positions revealed earlier at the Observatory telescope when you focused on the Edanna chamber (see figure 2-59). The cage lowers.

Fig. 2-59. Move the marbles in the Edanna podium's code-wheel to this configuration.

▲ Open the Edanna book.

▲ Touch the linking book panel to link to Edanna, the Nature Age.

Fig. 2-60. Edanna here we come!

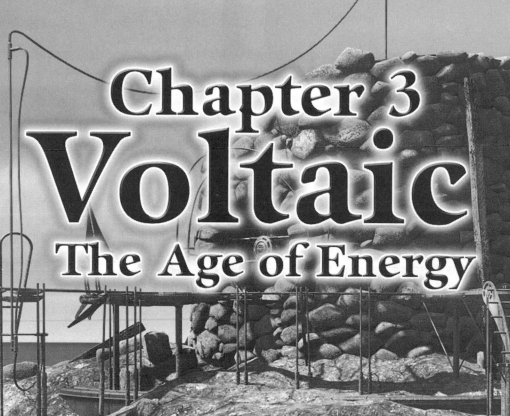

Chapter 3
Voltaic
The Age of Energy

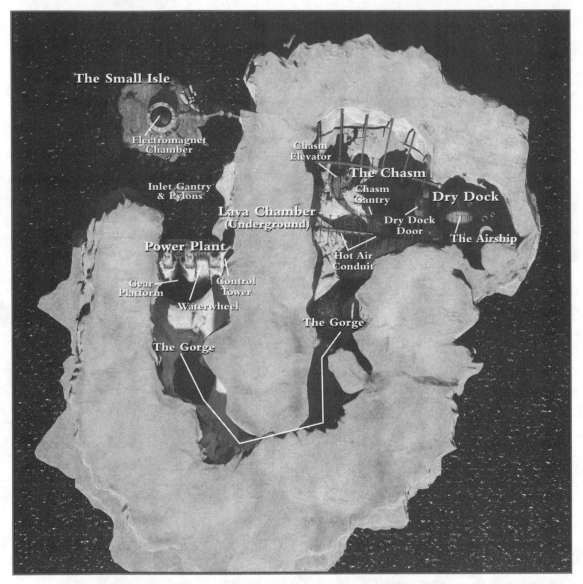

Fig. 3-1. Here's an overhead view of the Voltaic Age. Some primary structures, such as the Lava Chamber, lie underground, so they aren't visible here.

Welcome to Voltaic, the Age of Energy. The map of the island (see figure 3-1) reveals a U-shaped canyon lined by forbidding sandstone cliffs. Your task is to get power flowing to the Small Isle in the upper-left corner. To do so, you must harness, transform, or channel various forms of natural energy to activate a series of mechanisms.

Note: Your ultimate goal in each of the three Element Ages is the same: Find that Age's unique symbol and bring it back to J'nanin.

The Small Isle

Your Voltaic adventure begins on a metal catwalk over a tiny island, which we'll call the Small Isle. This isle sits at the mouth of an inlet that spills water down the main island's canyon. The catwalk leads to a stone building on the Small Isle. It also spans to the main island, where it curves into a crevasse through the cliff wall.

Fig. 3-2. This stone structure hunkers atop the Small Isle where you arrive in Voltaic.

- Proceed along the catwalk to the door of the stone building on the Small Isle.

- Try to open the door. Nothing happens. The lock mechanism attached to the door's handle needs power.

- Turn left to see the metal container; it looks like a shiny basketball with wings. Approach it.

Fig. 3-3. This conveniently placed book links right back to the Voltaic book chamber on J'nanin.

- ✏ Click on the container to open it, revealing a J'nanin linking book. This links back to the Voltaic book chamber. Use it only if you get stuck on this Age and want to explore elsewhere. (Of course, you won't get stuck if you stick with us!)

- ✏ Examine the area: the pylons and gantry tower rising from the inlet, the power plant's sluice gate just beyond the tower, and the route of the power cable.

Fig. 3-4. This power cable runs from the stone structure down into the water.

A thick electrical cable runs from the Small Isle's stone building to a metal pole at the end of the catwalk, then threads under the catwalk and disappears into the water. Just yards away, two metal pylons and a stone gantry tower rise from the inlet water; more cable runs from the far pylon toward a power plant farther up the canyon. In fact, the inlet gantry and pylons are part of an electrical power system that runs through the entire Age, delivering energy to various locations.

Fig. 3-5. Cross this catwalk to the main island.

◄ Follow the catwalk across the water and into the crevasse on the main island.

◄ At the first intersection (just before you emerge into the open chasm), turn right to see a narrow, red-lit tunnel.

◄ Follow the red-lit tunnel. Watch for another one of Saavedro's journal pages on the tunnel floor.

This journal entry starts at the beginning, as it were. Saavedro describes "the fog that eats my mind" (his madness) and the moment that helped him emerge from that fog: the arrival of Atrus on J'nanin.

◄ Proceed to the next intersection. You see a door just ahead. If you try the door, you discover it's jammed from the inside. (By Saavedro, perhaps?)

◄ Turn right to see a narrow, blue-lit tunnel.

◄ Follow the blue-lit tunnel to the power plant.

Power Plant

A hydroelectric power plant spans the length of a waterfall that drops from the ocean inlet into the canyon below. The plant has three sections: a two-story control tower, a long cylindrical waterwheel, and a gear platform that powers a turbine generator. Check out the map in figure 3-1. See how the inlet rocks split the falls into two separate spillways? One spillway runs under the waterwheel, one under the gear platform. A movable sluice gate directs water into only one spillway at a time.

The power plant is not producing electricity at the moment. Your goal is to activate the plant and thus generate power for other mechanisms in the Voltaic Age.

- ❦ Step out of the tunnel into the alcove.
- ❦ Turn left and step forward to examine the power flow diagram. (See figure 3-6.)

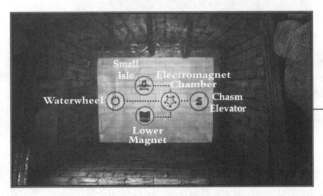

Fig. 3-6. Icons in this diagram indicate various mechanisms (labeled here) in the Age. A glowing icon means power is flowing to that mechanism.

When the power is on, the diagram's icons glow to depict the flow of electricity to various mechanisms around the island. (A lit icon means the designated mechanism is powered up.) At the moment, none of the diagram's icons are lit because the plant is not producing electricity.

Fig. 3-7. Climb this ladder to top of the control tower.

- ❦ Turn around and approach the ladder.
- ❦ Climb up the ladder to the top of the control tower (two clicks up).

Control Tower

Nice view! The Small Isle looms across the water to your right. So does the inlet gantry tower and its nearby pylons. The sluice gate and the cylindrical waterwheel lie directly below. Attached to the waterwheel are several rows of movable flaps called "vanes." When these vanes are deployed—that is, flipped open—and water is running under the waterwheel, the water pushes the vanes, causing the wheel to turn. The vanes are currently retracted, however.

Fig. 3-8. From the control tower you can see the sluice gate (at right) and the waterwheel (the cylinder below).

- Examine the control panel. The red wheel at right moves the sluice gate. Saavedro removed the other wheel, which had deployed the waterwheel's vanes.

- Turn the red wheel.

The sluice gate slides over to its far position, redirecting water under the waterwheel. Again, the vanes aren't deployed, so the wheel doesn't spin. Don't worry, though, you don't want it spinning just yet.

Fig. 3-9. Turn this red control wheel to move the sluice gate to the far side, letting water flow under the waterwheel. (Do this before you deploy the waterwheel's vanes!)

- Climb back down the ladder.
- Turn to face the metallic corridor (opposite the tunnel you emerged from).

This corridor runs the length of the waterwheel. As mentioned earlier, the waterwheel itself is a long cylindrical tube stretching from the control tower to the gear platform. You can see the gear platform at the other end of the corridor.

Gear Platform

- Proceed through the waterwheel's metallic corridor.

- Cross the gear platform and examine the round, forbidding security door. It resembles the one on the Small Isle building; like that one, its lock mechanism has no power, so you can't open it yet.

- Turn around and examine the platform.

Fig. 3-10. The security door off the gear platform is locked. It won't open until the turbine generator is producing power.

A massive gear sits horizontally just under the floor. This floor gear, when turning, powers a turbine generator, the island's source of electricity. To turn, the floor gear must be engaged with the huge waterwheel gear attached vertically to the end of the waterwheel. When the waterwheel turns, both gears spin, thus converting the wheel's kinetic energy into electricity.

The gears aren't spinning yet, nor are they engaged. The floor gear has been lowered to its release position. But a ladder runs down a nearby vertical shaft to a gear crank. This crank allows you to raise the floor gear so that it engages the waterwheel gear.

Fig. 3-11. This shaft leads down to a crank mechanism that can raise the floor gear.

- Step onto the gear platform, turn right, and approach the shaft.
- Climb down the ladder into the shaft.

Note: If the shaft is filled with water, the sluice gate is in the wrong setting. Go back to the control tower, climb the ladder, and turn the red control wheel to move the sluice gate so that water is diverted under the waterwheel rather than under the gear platform.

- At the bottom, push the red button to open the door and reveal the floor gear's emergency release mechanism.
- Step closer to the mechanism and click on the crank handle at left. This raises the floor gear, engaging it with the waterwheel gear.

Fig. 3-12. Turn the crank handle on the left side of this mechanism to raise the floor gear.

You cannot turn this crank while the waterwheel gear is in motion; the floor gear just grinds and drops back down, still disengaged. Thus, the two gears can be engaged only when (1) water is flowing under the waterwheel, *not* under the gear platform, and (2) the waterwheel's vanes are closed so the waterwheel does not turn.

Now that you have the gears engaged, it's time to open those vanes.

- Climb out of the shaft.
- Head back down the waterwheel's metallic corridor.

Waterwheel Corridor (Vanes)

- Walk down the metallic corridor, stopping just before you reach the control tower alcove.
- Turn right to see the damaged view-port.
- Click on the view-port for a close-up. You see a section of the waterwheel's vanes.

Fig. 3-13. Flip open the vanes manually, but only after you engage the big gears at the gear platform.

Tip: Closed vanes can be opened whether or not water is flowing over them; however, open vanes can be closed only if water is directed away from the waterwheel.

- Click on the vanes to manually open them. Voilà! The waterwheel begins to spin.

- Back away and turn left. Step into the alcove, then turn left again and examine the power flow diagram.

Newly lit icons on the diagram indicate that power flows from the plant's generator to a device somewhere beyond the gear platform. Let's track that power flow, shall we?

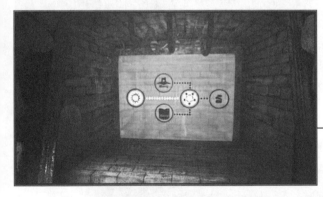

Fig. 3-14. Power now flows from the power plant's turbine generator to the electromagnet chamber.

- Walk down the metallic corridor. Just before you step onto the gear platform, note the engaged gears turning.

- Optional: Crawl down the shaft again and open the compartment to see the generator's gear mechanism spinning happily.

- Cross the gear platform to the security door.

Electromagnet Chamber

Fig. 3-15. The gear platform door can open once power lights up the lock mechanism.

- Aha! The security door's lock mechanism now glows with power. Click on it to open the door and see another shaft leading down.

- Climb down the shaft's ladder into the antechamber. At the bottom you see a passage at right, and an odd device with a view-screen at left—an imager.

- Approach the imager and click the button beneath the view-screen. It's another message from Saavedro. (See the following Note.)

Fig. 3-16. The imager in the antechamber plays another bitter message from Saavedro to Atrus.

- Follow the long passage that leads from the antechamber.

- Enter the electromagnet chamber.

Note: Each of the three Ages has an imager with a separate message from Saavedro. You can visit the Ages (and find the imagers) in any order. But the messages play in the same order regardless of the order you visit the Ages. So Saavedro's first message plays on the first imager you activate, whether on Voltaic, Amateria, or Edanna. The second message plays on the second imager you activate, no matter which Age; the same goes for the third message on the third imager you activate.

Fig. 3-17. The central cylinder houses a vast circuit array full of connectors that must be aligned for power to flow to other Voltaic locations.

Five platforms surround a big central cylinder. Inside the cylinder, three continuous strips of electrical circuits ring the cylinder's interior wall. Segments of these circuits are visible through apertures in the cylinder; the apertures can be found under the D'ni numerals etched at each platform (see figure 3-18). Your first look at the circuit configuration reveals disconnected wiring, which explains why the power flow from the generator stops here.

Note: The figure etched over each aperture station is a D'ni numeral. The numeral over the station at the bottom of the ladder is 1. As you circle counterclockwise around the cylinder, the stations are marked with the D'ni numerals 2, 3, 4, and 5.

- Climb down the ladder into the chamber.
- Click on the aperture station at the bottom of the ladder and examine its controls.

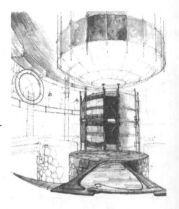

Fig. 3-18. This is the first aperture station on the cylinder, marked by the D'ni numeral 1. (See figure 3-20 for the final circuit settings for this aperture.)

Fig. 3-19. Here's a view through the aperture. Press the buttons on either side to rotate the corresponding circuit strip in that direction.

The circuit array features stationary connector pins at the very top and very bottom. Three movable strips of circuits are stacked between these pins. Buttons outside the aperture let you rotate each strip left or right. Your goal here is to line up connector pins until there are no unconnected circuits at any aperture station. You must rotate the strips in the same direction in order to solve this puzzle.

Specifically (and stay with us here): Every stationary connector pin at the top of the circuit array must connect to a pin on the top circuit strip. Every pin on the topmost strip must connect to a pin on the middle strip. Every pin on the middle strip must connect to a pin on the lower strip. And every pin on the lower strip must connect to a stationary connector pin at the bottom of the circuit array.

This probably sounds more complicated than it really is. Simply put, you must create an unbroken pathway for electricity to run from the stationary top pins through the circuit strips to the stationary bottom pins in *all five aperture views*. When this happens, electricity arcs from the circuit in the center of the room to the electromagnetic coils lining the chamber walls.

Note: Remember, when you move a circuit strip at one aperture, you are moving it in *all five* apertures. Also note that clicking any button 20 times moves that circuit strip completely around the cylinder once.

- Look into the aperture at station 1 (the one by the ladder). Click the top right-hand button as many times as it takes to move the row of pins on the uppermost circuit strip into alignment with both of the stationary pins above them.

- Once you find a position in which top row pins match up with the stationery pins above them, step away from aperture station 1, walk to station 2, and look into this aperture.

- Do the top row pins here line up with the stationary pins above them? If they don't, click the top right-hand button until these pins line up correctly. If they *do* line up, then step away from station 2, walk to station 3 and peer into this aperture.

- Continue to line up the topmost pins in the top strip with the stationary pins above them in all five stations until *every* station's top pins form an unbroken line from stationary pin to top pin.

✔ Then walk back to Station 1. Click the *bottom* right button as many times as it takes to move the row of pins on the bottommost circuit strip into alignment with the two stationary pins below them.

✔ When they match, move to the next station and check to see if all bottom pins line up. Continue clicking just the bottom right button until all bottom pins line up in all five aperture stations.

✔ Now, repeat this process with the middle row of circuits. Here, however, you must match the pins on the middle circuit strip with the top strip *and* the bottom strip pins. Again, you must form an unbroken line of connector pins from the top stationary pins to the bottom stationary pins.

✔ If you get really frustrated, go back to aperture 1 and check out figure 3-20 for the solution.

✔ When you succeed, you automatically step back and the aperture station slams shut. Electricity arcs across the top of the electromagnet chamber.

Note: Warning! Quick cheat solution follows. The first time you look into any aperture, rotate the top strip to the right 10 times, rotate the middle strip to the right two times, and rotate the bottom strip to the right four times.

Fig. 3-20. To solve the circuit puzzle, move the circuit strips to match this configuration in aperture 1.

✔ Go around the right side of the cylinder. Proceed past the first platform to the second one.

✔ Find another one of Saavedro's loose journal entries on the floor next to the cylinder.

✔ Open Saavedro's journal and read the new pages.

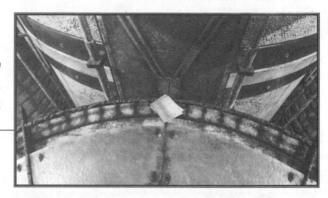

Fig. 3-21. Don't miss these journal pages left on the floor behind the electromagnet cylinder. Saavedro wants you to find them.

The tragedy of Saavedro's experience comes into sharper focus in these new journal passages. He recounts a near-encounter with Catherine during one of his excursions to Tomahna. The moment spawns painful memories of his own wife, Tamra, and their two daughters—all presumed dead. Saavedro writes of the dying of his home Age, Narayan, a place once sustained by the "Lattice Tree."

- Go back up the ladder, follow the tunnel to the next ladder, and climb up to the gear platform.

- Return through the waterwheel's metallic corridor to the alcove at the bottom of the power station's control tower.

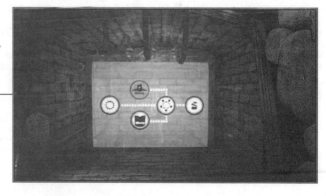

Fig. 3-22. Now the diagram indicates power flowing everywhere but one location on the Age.

- Examine the power flow diagram. The lit icons now indicate electricity flowing to all but one mechanism on the island.

- Backtrack through the blue-lit and red-lit tunnels until you reach the big crevasse. Then turn right and follow the catwalk into the chasm.

The Chasm

The chasm is a large circular canyon with a narrow gorge branching off to the south (as seen on the map in figure 3-1). The canyon was carved by a whirlpool; water flows down through the gorge from the inlet's waterfall. Note the series of tall metal pylons that thread their way up the gorge. These pylons support a thick power cable running from the power plant. When it reaches the chasm, this cable makes a 90-degree loop around a stone gantry tower, and then disappears behind a massive dome-like door.

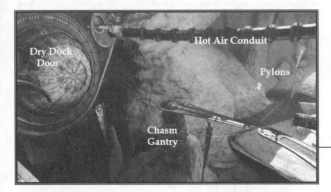

Fig. 3-23. Welcome to the chasm. A power cable strung on pylons (far right) runs down the gorge, curves around the gantry tower platform (center), and heads for the dry dock door (far left). The segmented pipe (top) is a hot-air conduit.

Fig. 3-24. This big, circular, segmented door releases the airship from its dry dock.

- Follow the catwalk all the way across the open chasm, passing a T-intersection and the dry dock door to your right.

- At the catwalk's end, look down to find the ladder, then descend. You end up in the airship dry dock.

Airship Dry Dock

The airship hangs in a cavern carved into the east side of the chasm. (See the map in figure 3-1.) A massive, segmented door seals the cave entrance. At one time the airship could be reached via a catwalk, but Saavedro destroyed this access, making it impossible to enter the airship from inside the dry dock. Your goal: Get the airship out of dry dock and to the gantry platform in the chasm.

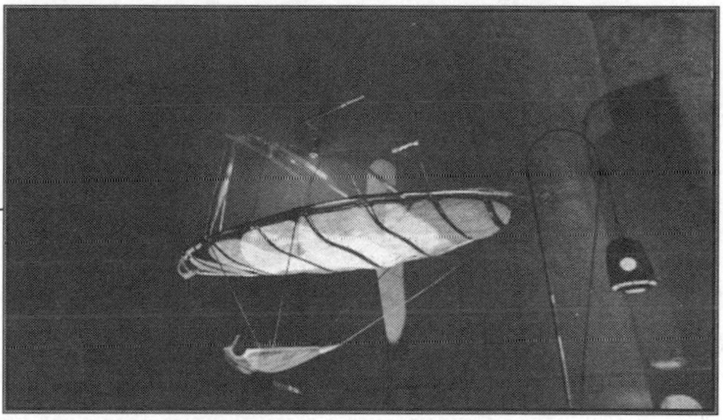

Fig. 3-25. Even when deflated, the airship is impressive.

The airship is a hot-air balloon with a gondola. Notice that the balloon is not inflated. A series of pipes connects the balloon to a hot-air conduit on the far side of the cave. The pipes run from the conduit through a three-tiered system of pressure valves housed in the tall tower just ahead.

Unfortunately, no air flows through the pipes right now. Guess what your next task is?

- Cross the lower catwalk to a platform with four valve wheels and a gauge.

- Examine the valve system.

Fig. 3-26. These valves control the air pressure for inflating the airship. No hot air is flowing, however.

This lower tier of valves feeds hot air down the air pipe (see figure 3-27) that leads to the airship's balloon. Each valve releases a set amount of pressure. Two more tiers of valves sit above you in the tower—thus, three tiers, four valves to a tier, twelve valves total.

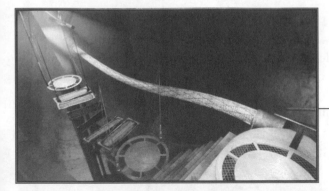

Fig. 3-27. This pipe directs hot air from the valve system to the airship's balloon. Note how Saavedro has destroyed the catwalk to the airship.

◄ If you experiment with the valves, nothing happens; no air flows through them right now.

◄ As you examine the valves, you stand on a pneumatic lift that provides access to all three tiers of valves in the valve tower. But if you pull the lift handle at lower left, nothing happens. Again, no air is feeding through the system right now to provide pneumatic power.

◄ Turn around and step onto the platform beyond the lift. Just ahead, note Saavedro's damage to the catwalk that leads to the airship.

◄ Turn right to see the spars of a maintenance ladder rising up between the cave wall and the valve tower. Climb these spars to a metal staircase, then climb the staircase to the top: the juncture where the hot air conduit feeds into the valve tower.

Fig. 3-28. Find the maintenance ladder just around the corner from the valve station. Climb it to the maintenance hatch at the top.

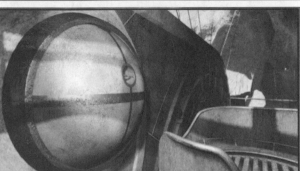

- Turn right and climb onto the small platform.

- Pick up another page of Saavedro's journal. This entry gives us Saavedro polishing a cavern wall and mixing paints in an endeavor to show Atrus "the pain his family has caused."

- Approach the dome-shaped maintenance hatch and click on its handle to rotate it open.

- Crawl through the hatch and veer left to crawl atop the hot-air conduit (the long segmented pipe spanning the chasm).

- Cross the chasm on the hot-air conduit. On the other side, you find another hatch. This leads into a ventilation duct.

- Open and enter the hatch, then crawl down the ventilation duct through the darkness until you are atop a round grate.

- Click on the grate to open it.

- Drop down into the lava chamber control room.

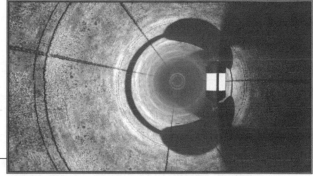

Fig. 3-29. The ventilation duct is dark and spooky, but plunge forward to the grate that opens downward.

Lava Chamber

Hot enough for you? This lava chamber provides the superheated air needed to inflate the airship. The chamber features two areas: a two-level control room (where you are now) and a lava containment center. A giant intake fan draws hot air into a conduit (the segmented pipe you walked across the chasm) and funnels it to the dry dock's valve tower.

You dropped from the ventilation duct into the top level of the control room. A shaft with a ladder leads down to the bottom level. Behind you, a window overlooks the lava containment center, a large room that contains, oddly enough, lava. In front of you is a door.

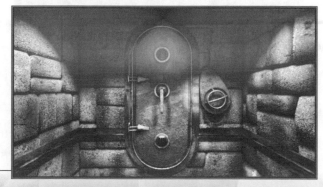

Fig. 3-30. Open this door to the tunnel system for quicker access from the lava chamber to the rest of the island.

- Step toward the door and click on the latch at right to slide it up.

- Open the door.

This tunnel intersection looks familiar. You passed here earlier, but this door was locked. Now you know why—the work of Saavedro, of course. The blue-lit tunnel runs to the power station; the red-lit tunnel runs back out to the crevasse connecting the Small Isle and the chasm.

- Turn and approach the control room window.

- Locate the fan on the wall at upper right.

Fig. 3-31. Here's the view from the control room window. See the fan at upper right?

That fan pumps hot air down the conduit. But it's turned off at the moment. Its control switch is on the wall just below the fan, accessible via a catwalk. But you can't see the switch yet; it's hidden behind the catwalk's vertical end-piece. Can we reach it?

- Go down the ladder to the bottom floor of the control room.

- Look through the door's view-port to see the lava filling the containment center.

Fig. 3-32. Molten lava fills the containment room when you first arrive.

Hot lava could be an impediment—you need to drain it before opening this door.

The containment center has two large gates on opposite walls: one gate lets lava flow in, the other lets lava drain out. The gates can be

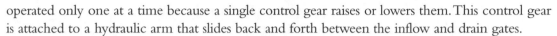
operated only one at a time because a single control gear raises or lowers them. This control gear is attached to a hydraulic arm that slides back and forth between the inflow and drain gates.

To complicate matters further, when positioned at either lava gate, the control gear also raises or lowers the catwalk that (when raised to its highest setting) reaches the fan control switch. So raising or lowering either lava gate simultaneously raises or lowers the catwalk.

Therefore, the goal is to manipulate the catwalk and the lava gates so that you:

1. Empty the room of lava.

2. Reach the fan control and turn it on.

3. Refill the room with lava to blow hot air down the conduit.

- Go back to the top floor of the control room.

- Approach the control wheel at the window. Note that Saavedro has jammed the center groove by wedging in a bolt.

Fig. 3-33. Saavedro's sabotage (the wedged bolt) limits your options at the control room's control wheel.

The red knob activates the control gear in the containment room. Rotating the red knob around the outer groove of the wheel turns the control gear in the direction (clockwise or counter-clockwise) you rotated the knob. Sliding the knob across the center groove moves the hydraulic arm (and thus the control gear) from one lava gate to the other. But, as mentioned, Saavedro jammed the center groove on this control wheel.

- Click and hold on the red knob.

- Drag it in a counterclockwise direction around the outer groove until it clicks twice, and then release.

The knob makes one counterclockwise rotation. Through the window you see the control gear (now at far right) turn counterclockwise. As it turns, it simultaneously lowers the catwalk and lifts the drain gate, clearing the room of lava. Now you can enter through the bottom floor of the control room. (Note that you can see the fan control switch on the wall beneath the fan.)

Fig. 3-34. The lava containment room and its main features.

- Go back down the ladder.
- Open the door and enter the containment room, now lava free.
- Turn left and step onto the catwalk.
- Examine the surroundings.

See the fan control switch on the wall just under the fan? Now find the circular hole in the catwalk's vertical end–piece. The hole is designed to match up with the fan switch, so you must raise the catwalk high enough to reach the switch through the hole.

And say… is that a *painting* on the drain gate to the right?

Fig. 3-35. The catwalk in the lava containment room has the same control mechanism as the one in the control room. But this one's not damaged!

- Approach the control wheel on the catwalk. This second control wheel works the same as the first, but the center groove is not jammed. So you can rotate *or* slide the red knob to manipulate the control gear.
- Move the red knob in a clockwise direction. The control gear rotates clockwise, simultaneously raising the catwalk and lowering the lava drain gate at right.

Fig. 3-36. Slide the red knob through the center groove to move the hydraulic arm (with the control gear) from side to side.

◤ Now slide the red knob to the left through the center groove. The hydraulic arm moves the control gear to the left side, engaging it to the large gear that moves the lava inflow gate.

◤ Step forward and then examine the painting on the drain gate.

Fig. 3-37. Examine this disturbing painting on the lava drain gate.

The work seems to depict a society aflame, at war with itself, fighting while two young men in a hovering gondola—Sirrus and Achenar, no doubt—flee the dying Age with bags full of riches, callously toasting their success at wreaking havoc. In the right foreground, a man stands apart from the strife with his family, a woman and two children.

Clearly the man is Saavedro. And this painting is a message to Atrus.

◤ Go back to the control wheel.

◤ Rotate the red knob counterclockwise to simultaneously raise both the catwalk and the inflow gate. Lava flows into the room below. More importantly, the hole in the catwalk's vertical end-piece now reveals the fan control switch.

◤ Step forward to the fan switch and turn it on.

Fig. 3-38. Halfway there! Now you've exposed the fan controls.

- Go back to the control wheel and rotate the red knob clockwise. This lowers the catwalk one level and closes the lava inflow gate. (If you look up, you see the fan now spinning.)

- Slide the red knob to the right to move the control gear to the right side.

- Rotate the red knob counterclockwise to simultaneously open the lava drain gate (emptying the room of lava, thank goodness) and lower the catwalk. Whew!

Good! Now the fan is blowing and the drain gate is open. When lava flows through the room again, the fan will push superheated air down the conduit to the airship dry dock. It's time to make that happen. But don't leave the containment room yet! Remember, up in the control room, the red knob won't slide because of Saavedro's sabotage. So, you must shift the control gear over to the inflow gate before you go.

- Important! Slide the red knob to the left to move the control gear over to the inflow gate side.

- Exit the lava containment room.

- Climb the ladder back to the control room's second level.

- Approach the control wheel and rotate the red knob counterclockwise. This raises both the inflow gate and the catwalk, allowing lava to flow freely through the room.

- Now head back to the dry dock! First, look straight up to find the ventilation duct opening. Click on it to enter the duct.

- Crawl through the tunnel to the hatch and exit the duct.

Fig. 3-39. Exit the lava chamber via the ceiling duct and then cross the chasm again, using the hot air conduit as your bridge to the dry dock.

- Cross the chasm on the hot air conduit.

- Crawl through the maintenance hatch, and then climb down the stairs and the maintenance ladder to the dry dock platform.

Airship Dry Dock (Valve Puzzle)

Hot air is flowing down the conduit, but the airship isn't inflating! Why? As with any balloon, the air must be forced in with pressure. The conduit channeling hot air from the lava chamber enters the dry dock's valve tower and splits into three sets of valves that supply pressure for this job.

If too little pressure is sent through the valves, of course, the airship doesn't inflate. But if too *much* pressure goes through the valves, a release valve automatically opens, venting hot air before it reaches the airship. Therefore, to inflate the airship you must open and close specific valves, adjusting the pressure to an exactly specified level.

Remember, there are three tiers of valves; each tier contains four valves. When you first arrive at the valve tower after solving the lava chamber puzzle, all valves are open (that is, venting hot air) except one. That one, on the bottom tier, has been jammed shut by someone who just may have long straggly hair and a grudge the size of Greenland.

- Approach the lower tier of valves. Again, three valves are open (venting hot air) and one is closed.

- Examine the pressure gauge.

The black needle indicates a current pressure of 10; zero is the line between the blue and red zones, and the needle moves counterclockwise as air pressure rises. See the red line marking 19 units of pressure at the upper left? That's the exact air pressure needed to inflate the airship without tripping the release valve. So you must open valves until you hit 19.

Fig. 3-40. When a valve cap is up and venting air (as seen here), the valve is "open."

Valve Tower: The Elevator

But, of course, there's a catch. The valve tower elevator is pneumatic; it needs air pressure to operate. The gauge's pressure reading must be in the yellow zone (equal to or greater than 22) for the elevator to reach the middle tier of valves. The reading must be in the red zone (greater than or equal to 49) to reach the top tier. So to get to higher tiers, you must initially increase pressure far above the 19 needed to inflate the airship.

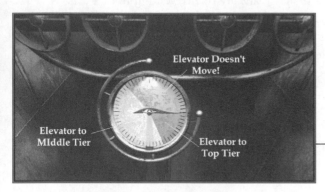

Fig. 3-41. A black indicator needle in the red zone means the elevator can reach the top tier. A yellow reading reaches the middle tier, but blue won't get you off the ground.

Setting the Valves

Total pressure can range from 0 to 60 units. Each lower tier valve provides 10 units of pressure. Each middle tier valve provides 4 units of pressure. Each top tier valve provides 1 unit of pressure. Again, when you first arrive after solving the lava chamber puzzle, all valve caps but one are open—that is, 11 of the 12 caps are up and hot air is escaping.

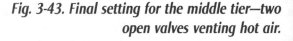

- Again, note that one valve cap on the lower tier (the far right valve) is closed. If you try to open it by turning its valve wheel, nothing happens; the wheel is jammed.

- Turn the valve wheels to close the other three valve caps on the lower tier. This raises pressure from 10 to 40 units, pushing the gauge needle into the yellow zone—enough to get the elevator up to the middle tier.

- Click on the elevator handle and drag it all the way to the right. The elevator rises to the middle tier.

- Close three of the venting valves on the middle tier. This raises pressure by 12, pushing the gauge needle into the red zone, from 40 to 52—enough to reach the top tier.

- Pull the elevator handle to the right again to ride up to the top tier.

- Close just one valve on the top tier. This raises total pressure by 1, from 52 to 53.

Fig. 3-42. Final setting for the top tier—three open valves venting hot air.

- Pull the elevator handle to the left and ride down to the middle tier.

- Open one more valve, so that a total of two valves are open and venting air. This reduces total pressure by 4, from 53 to 49.

Fig. 3-43. Final setting for the middle tier—two open valves venting hot air.

- Pull the elevator handle to the left and ride down to the bottom tier.

- Open the three valves that are not jammed. This reduces total pressure by 30, from 49 to 19.

Fig. 3-44. Final setting for the bottom tier—three open valves venting hot air. (The jammed valve stays closed.)

The total pressure output is now 1 unit from the top tier of valves, 8 from the middle tier of valves, and 10 units from the bottom tier of valves: a total of 19, the number indicated by the red line on the gauge. (The black indicator needle should be on the red line now.)

- Go around the corner to the release valve.
- Turn the release valve to pump the pressurized hot air into the airship.

Fig. 3-45. After you get a pressure reading of 19, turn this release valve wheel to fill the airship.

Note: If there's not enough pressure to inflate the airship when you turn the final release valve wheel, nothing happens. If there's too much pressure, the release valve blows, forcing you to try again.

Watch the airship inflate, rise, and sail forward. After a short flight, the ship halts at the closed dry dock doors. Next step: Let's open those doors.

Fig. 3-46. And there she goes! But she doesn't go far.

- Step across the elevator platform and cross the catwalk (underneath the airship) to the far side of the dry dock cavern.

- Climb the ladder and follow the upper walkway into the chasm.

The Chasm Gantry

Time to open that big, segmented dry dock door and free the airship. The door's release lever is one level down, at the end of the stone gantry platform. An electric elevator connects the upper walkway level (where you are now) to the lower walkway that leads to the lever.

Note: If you haven't solved the puzzles in both the power plant and the electromagnet chamber, the elevator won't have power and you can't access the gantry.

Fig. 3-47. Cross the upper walkway to this intersection, then turn left and follow the curve to the elevator.

- Follow the upper walkway across the chasm to the T-intersection.

- Turn left and follow the curve to the chasm elevator.

Fig. 3-48. This corkscrew elevator connects the chasm's upper and lower walkways.

- Step onto the elevator.

- Pull the handle to ride the elevator down to the lower walkway.

- When the elevator reaches bottom, turn around to find more of Saavedro's journal pages on the ground. This entry recounts the insidious treachery of Sirrus and Achenar as they incite a generational dispute on Narayan regarding time-honored traditions of "the Tree."

Fig. 3-49. Pull that lever at the end of the gantry platform to open the dry dock doors and release the airship.

- Follow the lower walkway to the dry dock door release lever.

- Pull the release lever; the door opens. The airship emerges, floats along the cable, bumps against the gantry platform's walkway, and comes to a halt.

Note that the airship's weight pushes the gantry walkway slightly forward, away from the elevator walkway. After this happens, you cannot access the elevator again; your only choice is to board the airship. But that's exactly what you want to do.

Fig. 3-50. The airship stops at the end of the gantry walkway. Climb aboard.

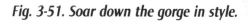

- Walk to the airship and climb in.
- Pull the airship release handle in the front of the gondola.

Fig. 3-51. Soar down the gorge in style.

Now sit back for a scenic joyride through the winding twists and turns of Voltaic's gorge. As you round the corner of the gorge, you see the power plant's waterwheel spinning ahead of you. The airship soars majestically over the wheel, floats along the inlet, and bumps to a stop at the first pylon.

- Exit the airship onto the gantry platform.
- Examine the gantry and pylons.

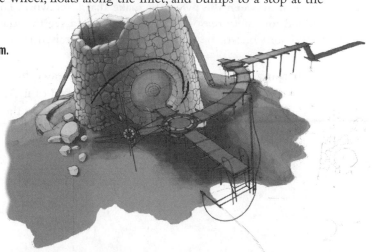

The Inlet Gantry & Pylons

Look under the airship. See that pole jutting from the first pylon? It connects to the power cable from the plant generator, and travels under the airship, but doesn't connect to the second pylon. So, the power connection from the generator via the pylons to the Small Isle is broken here.

Fig. 3-52. When you pull the gantry lever, the airship pushes this pole to connect the inlet pylons.

- Proceed to the lever at the end of the gantry platform. This lever connects to a brake that prevents the airship from moving forward.

- Pull the lever and watch the automatic sequence that follows.

Note: The lever on the gantry platform was installed to control the levitating island. The circuit is broken between the pylons to make that lever work. The inlet gantry and the lever were added for safety reasons, so operators could see the island before raising it. (You wouldn't want someone to be on the island while it raised.)

You swing around to see the airship, now released from the brake, moving forward. As it moves, its weight pushes the gantry platform ahead of it. At the same time, the mechanism that holds the airship onto the cables below it lifts and drags the pole into its proper position on the second pylon.

Fig. 3-53. When the pole clicks into place to connect the inlet pylons, electricity flows to the Small Isle.

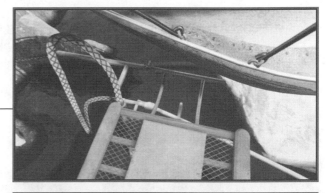

Fig. 3-54. Now that's impressive.

When this connection is complete, electricity flows through the circuit to the Small Isle. You swing around to see the isle break free of the ground! Wow! It levitates into the air—lifted, of course, by the magnetic force of two powerful electromagnets repelling each other in the chamber beneath the isle. The force also captures shards of rock and dirt, suspending them in a spiral between island and ground.

Remember the small electromagnet on Saavedro's work desk in the Observatory?

- Walk back to the airship, climb inside, and pull the release handle. The craft floats to the now levitated Small Isle.

- When you arrive, exit the airship onto the walkway.

Fig. 3-55. Now that power flows to the Small Isle door, you can open it and enter the stone building.

Notice that the metal container holding the J'nanin linking book has dropped down to make room for the airship; the book's no longer accessible. But you don't need it now. (Never did, in fact, if you're using this guide!) The glowing green light on the stone building's door indicates power now flows here.

Fig. 3-56. Climb down this long vertical shaft.

- Click on the door's lock mechanism. The door drops, revealing a small stone room with a ladder leading down a long vertical shaft.

- Enter the room and climb down the ladder to the bottom of the shaft.

- Click on the wheel on the floor.

Fig. 3-57. The Energy symbol literally floats in the air, suspended by magnetic force. You automatically record the symbol on a page.

The metal door slides apart, revealing a vertiginous view of the electromagnet chamber far below! Between the isle and the ground, floating debris has formed a symbol—the special Energy symbol you must take back to J'nanin. You automatically record the symbol on a blank page, which then goes into your inventory.

- Look up to see the cabinet doors in the wall directly ahead.

- Open the cabinet. Out pops another J'nanin linking book. This one, however, links more conveniently into the second floor of the Observatory.

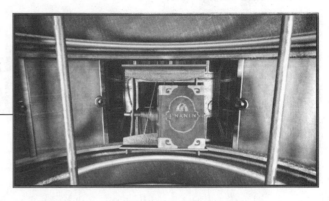

Fig. 3-58. Use this newly revealed book to link back to the J'nanin Observatory.

✍ Open the J'nanin book.

✍ Touch the animated linking panel to return to J'nanin.

Back to J'nanin

When you return to J'nanin from Voltaic with the Energy symbol, you link directly into the second floor of the Observatory.

✍ Approach the imaging table.

✍ Take your sketch of the Energy symbol from inventory and put it on the imaging table.

Fig. 3-59. Take the Energy symbol sketch from inventory and place it on the imaging table.

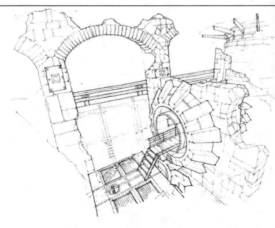

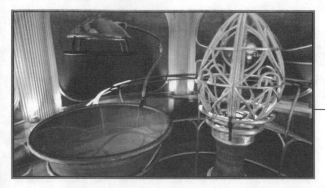

Fig. 3-60. The cams rotate, bringing the cage up out of the pit.

The imager projects the sketch downward, raising a three-dimensional representation of the symbol from a cam beneath the table. Another cam drops down, imprinting the 3-D symbol on its elastic surface. Then the cams rotate, manipulating the cage mechanism.

If you're following this walkthrough, Voltaic is the first Element Age you visit. Thus, placing the journal page on the imaging table lifts the cage out of the pit. When it locks into place directly across from you, another hologram projector message from Saavedro plays on the ceiling. (See the Note here.) Again, he speaks angrily of Atrus' sons, how their lies subverted the "traditions keeping Narayan alive." He also mentions the Lattice Trees that seem central to his Age's survival.

Fig. 3-61. Saavedro has another message for Atrus before sending him off for the remaining Age symbols.

Note: Remember you can bring back symbols from the Ages *in any order*. When placed on the imaging table, each symbol activates some aspect of the cage mechanism in the pit, then triggers a hologram message from Saavedro. Whether from Voltaic, Amateria, or Edanna, the first symbol placed on the imaging table raises the cage from the pit, the second symbol opens the cage, and the third symbol extends a ramp to the cage. Saavedro's messages play in the same order regardless of the order you solve the Ages.

- Once you bring back the first Age symbol and use it on the imaging table, the blue button thereafter triggers Saavedro's second message ("Not so easy, is it, Atrus?") until another Age symbol is retrieved and placed on the table.

- Go to the doors and exit the Observatory onto the high bridge.

- Solve the next linking book puzzle. In this walkthrough, we'll go to Amateria next. See "Getting from J'nanin to Amateria" in Chapter 2, J'nanin: The Lesson Age.

Fig. 3-62. Exit the Observatory to seek the next linking book.

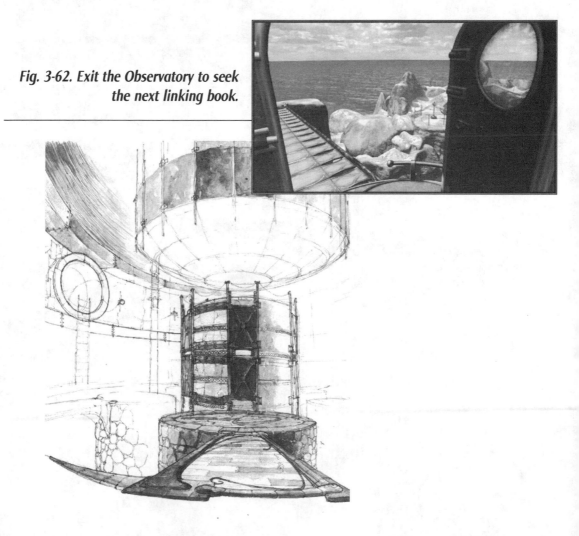

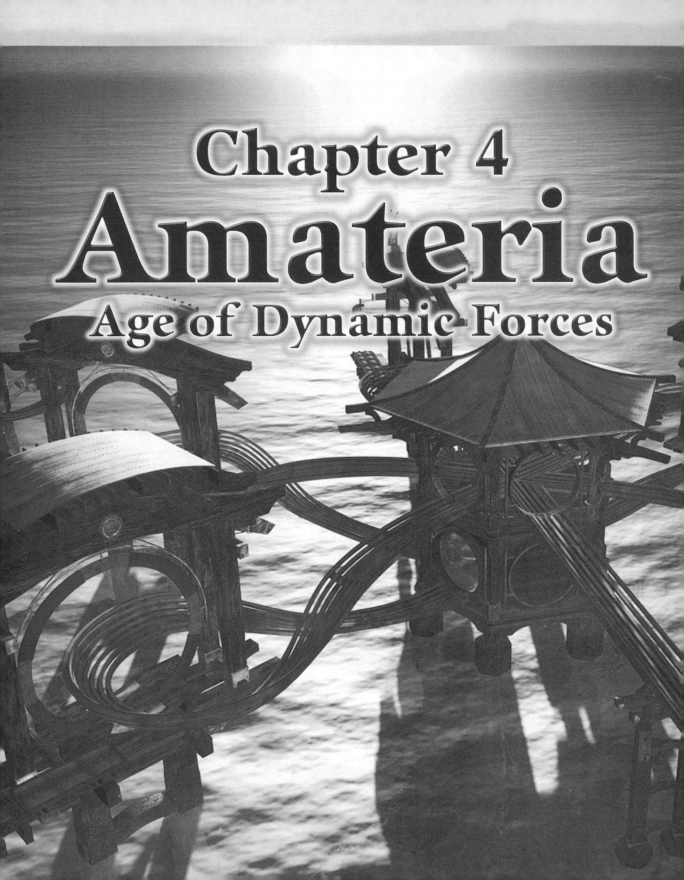

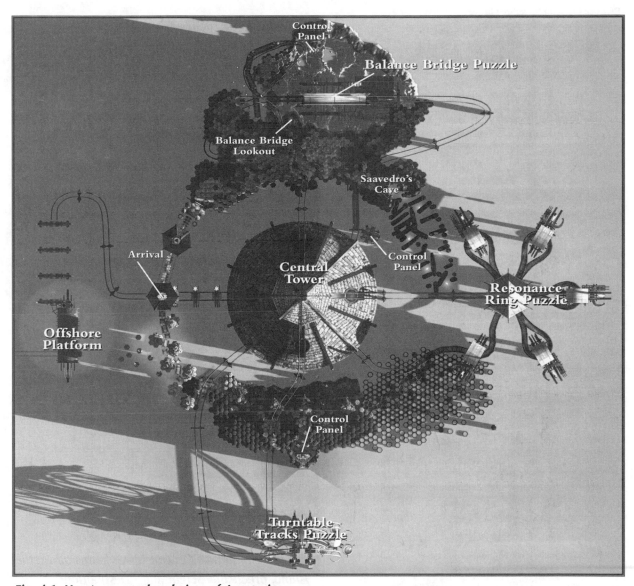

Fig. 4-1. Here's an overhead view of Amateria.

Amateria looks like a big, haunted amusement park ride, doesn't it? Apparently, Atrus wanted his boys to enjoy themselves while learning about Dynamic Forces. Elevated tracks run left, right, twist, and turn. Look at Amateria's layout in figure 4-1. Four structures, one at each compass point, surround a Central Tower. The north structure is the Balance bridge Puzzle; east is the Resonance Ring Puzzle; south is the Turntable Track Puzzle; and west is a mysterious, unnamed offshore platform.

Note: Your ultimate goal in each of the three "Element Ages" is the same: find that Age's unique symbol, then bring it back to the J'nanin Observatory.

Tracks run from the Central Tower to each structure, move through the structure in some fashion, and then run back to the Central Tower. The track's connection, however, is incomplete in some way in each structure. Your overall goal in Amateria is to complete this circuit of track for each structure.

Arrival: Pagoda Walkway

You arrive in Amateria inside a small wooden pagoda just as a flash of lightning lights up the distance. A slatted wooden bridge extends away from you, toward a second small pagoda.

Fig. 4-2. This offshore platform rises from the water just across from your point of arrival. Note how the tracks end at the first of three support columns.

Fig. 4-3. Amateria's Central Tower looms above the island, practically screaming, "Destination!"

◎ Swivel to your left. A set of tracks heads out over the water, curving right and then back, ending at the first of three columns. To the left of these columns is an unusual offshore structure.

◎ Turn to view a large roofed structure: the Central Tower. A wooden bridge extends to it.

◎ Step toward the tower. Your path is soon blocked by a gap in the wooden bridge.

◎ Turn left and examine the console before you.

Fig. 4-4. This hexagonal code box seems linked to the bridge that extends to the Central Tower.

A series of stone hexagons form an unusual pattern on the console. If you click any stone, it depresses. But if you click to zoom away, they reset. Obviously, this is some sort of code box.

◎ Step back to where you linked in and turn right. Proceed down the slatted wooden bridge to the next small pagoda.

◎ A J'nanin linking book sits on a podium here, should you need to return to the Lesson Age. (You won't if you follow us.)

Fig. 4-5. An emergency J'nanin linking book sits in one of the walkway pagodas.

◎ Continue walking across the next slatted bridge until you reach a tunnel formed by Amateria's towering basalt columns. A chain-link guardrail directs you to a set of hexagonal steps leading downward.

◎ Go down the curving stairs. They end up in a tunnel lit by two sources: fire marble lanterns carved into the columns, and glowing crystal fragments scattered along the cavern floor.

◎ Walk through the tunnel until you reach an opening to the left. Threatening storm clouds roil over the water in the distance. Look up to see more curving track just above the opening. Where does it lead?

○ Continue down the tunnel until you reach a fork in the path. The left fork leads to a wooden walkway. For now, take the right-hand fork.

○ An elevator shaft is carved into the basalt to the left. Board the wooden elevator and pull the lever to ride to the top.

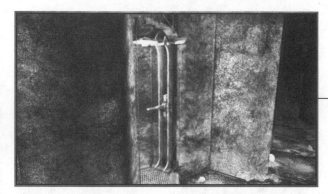

Fig. 4-6. Ride this elevator up to the Balance Bridge Lookout.

Balance Bridge

The elevator deposits you on a lookout ledge atop the caverns. Here, you get a close-up view of the massive Balance Bridge mechanism. Looping tracks curve around a basalt column and then run through a metal half-pipe bridge. The bridge balances atop an axle connecting two gearwheels. This axle is a fulcrum, set exactly in the middle of the bridge. If you roll the gearwheels, you can move the fulcrum to different points under the bridge, changing the distribution of weight.

Fig. 4-7. This half-pipe bridge balances on a fulcrum. A pair of gearwheels can roll the fulcrum forward and back under the bridge.

The Lookout

◎ Step out of the elevator and walk to the end of the lookout ramp.

◎ Examine the bridge. Note that something resembling a sling or hammock hangs from one end of the bridge. (See figure 4-8.) This is a "catch-basket"; you'll see how it works in a minute.

◎ Zoom in on the sphere that's sitting at the top of the looping track.

Fig. 4-8. Note the sling-like basket (circled here) hanging from this near end of the bridge.

Interesting. The sphere is divided into sections or wedges. From here you can see four of them. Three of these sections are made of wood, and one is made of crystal. Do these substances remind you of something you may have seen earlier? How about Saavedro's collection of balances in his Observatory?

Fig. 4-9. What a ball! Three parts wood, one part crystal.

◎ Return to the elevator.

◎ Before pulling the lever to go back down, look around carefully. Saavedro has left another journal entry here for you to find.

◎ Read the new entry. *Carnivorous hybrid? Grafts?* Sounds kind of ominous.

◎ Take the elevator back down.

◎ Exit the elevator and go right, retracing your steps to the fork in the path.

◎ Turn right to step outside the basalt cavern and follow the wooden walkway to the Balance Bridge control panel.

Control Panel

Outside the cavern you can see that the Balance Bridge sits above a honeycomb of glowing, geyser-formed paint pots. A control panel sits on a cross-shaped wooden platform. Mineral deposits on the other side of the platform form a walkway leading to a hut underneath the massive fulcrum bridge.

Fig. 4-10. The control panel at lower left operates the fulcrum bridge mechanism.

◎ Walk up to the control panel and pull the long-handled lever at left. Immediately the platform rises up, giving you a better view of the fulcrum bridge.

◎ Look closely at the multicolored sphere sitting on the rail.

This side of the sphere displays four more cross sections. All four are made of wood. So the sphere consists of seven wood sections and one crystal section. Let's flash back a moment to Saavedro's room in the J'nanin Observatory. The balances there revealed the following weight relationships:

1 metal sphere = 4 crystal spheres
1 crystal sphere = 4 wood spheres

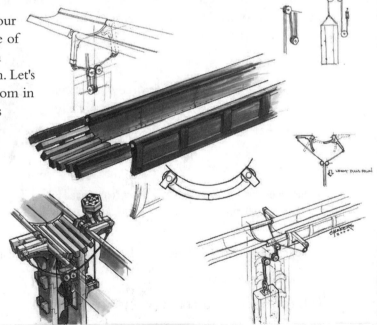

Fig. 4-11. This balance back in the J'nanin Observatory demonstrates that crystal is four times the weight of wood.

Thus the crystal section of the ball on the rail weighs the same as four wood sections. In terms of "wood weight," then, the multicolored ball on the rail weighs the same as 7 + 4 = 11 sections of wood. We'll call its total weight "11 wood."

- Experiment with the three sliding pegs on the control panel to determine their relationship to the massive fulcrum gearwheel. Listing the pegs in order from the top:

- Left, left, right sets the fulcrum to the far left.

- Left, right, left sets the fulcrum in the middle of the bridge.

- Right, left, left sets the fulcrum to the far right.

- Pull the console lever at right.

Fig. 4-12. The ice sphere from the Central Tower knocks the colored sphere into the bridge's catch-basket (circled here)...

Fig. 4-13. ...then shatters as it tries to cross the bridge. Looks like you need more weight on the left end of the Balance Bridge.

Watch as a crystalline ice sphere from the Central Tower swings around the upper track. This ice sphere clips the multicolored sphere as it passes, knocking it down a separate track that loops around the basalt column at right. The colored sphere reaches the bridge first, dropping into the catch-basket and pulling down the right-hand end of the bridge. Immediately after that, the ice sphere arrives, tries to cross the Balance Bridge, and shatters into pieces.

No matter where you move the fulcrum, you get the same results. Clearly, you need more counterweight on the left end of the bridge to keep it level. But how?

- ◎ Pull the long handled lever again to return to the ground.

- ◎ Walk along the ridge of mineral deposits. As you approach the hut-like room, look up at the bridge. (See figure 4-14.) Note that a rope hangs from this end, too, and drops through a hole in the roof of the hut.

- ◎ Continue until you reach a sliding door. Click to open it.

- ◎ Go through the doorway to enter the weight room.

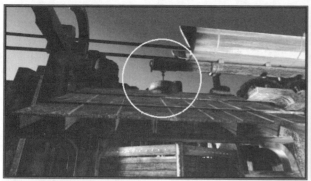 

Fig. 4-14. A rope hanging from the end of the bridge drops down through the hut's roof and into the Weight Room below.

Weight Room

A wooden balance hangs by a rope from the Balance Bridge (the half-pipe bridge) above. Wedges of crystal, metal, and wood lie on a bench along the back of the room. The hanging balance is a counterweight; it hangs on the opposite end of the bridge from the catch-basket that catches the multicolored ball.

Fig. 4-15. Place wedges from the bench (left) onto the wooden balance (right) to create enough counterweight.

As originally designed by Atrus, the puzzle solution was to place wedges onto the hanging wooden platform until the counterbalance matched the weight of the multicolored ball—that is, the equivalent of 11 wedges of wood. With both ends of the Balance Bridge in balance, the ice sphere could roll across and return to the Central Tower. But Saavedro smashed many of the wedges, making it impossible to achieve a one-to-one weight ratio. So you'll have to use the fulcrum controls outside on the console and do a little easy math.

Once again, a device back in Saavedro's J'nanin room hints at how to proceed. Remember the hanging stick figures next to the hammock? That miniature fulcrum toy featured two fixed weights attached to one end and exactly half that amount attached to the other. Back then we suggested you examine it to discover how to achieve balance despite the uneven distribution of weight—in that case, a 2 to 1 distribution.

Fig. 4-16. Saavedro's crude device back in J'nanin showed where to place the fulcrum to achieve balance with a 2 to 1 weight ratio.

Guess what? You need the same 2 to 1 distribution of weight on the Balance Bridge, with the fulcrum positioned in the same place as on the toy. Because the colored sphere on the tracks weighs the equivalent of 11 wood wedges, you need a balance weight of 22 wood.

Remember that the bottom half of the balance is all wood, so you're starting with a weight of 4 wood. Here's the solution:

◎ Add 2 wood wedges to increase the weight of the balance from 4 wood to 6 wood.

◎ Add one metal wedge to get a weight of 22 wood.

Fig. 4-17. Here's the combination of weights you want on the balance—2 wood, 1 metal.

Again, metal is four times heavier than crystal, which is four times heavier than wood. So the metal wedge is 16 times heavier than wood—1 metal wedge weighs 16 wood. This increases the balance platform's weight to 6 + 16 = 22 wood—twice the weight of the multicolored sphere. Now let's move the fulcrum to balance the Balance Bridge.

◎ Exit the Weight Room.

◎ Walk back to the Balance Bridge control panel.

Adjusting the Fulcrum

◎ Pull the lever to raise the console platform.

◎ Slide the bottom peg to the right. (See figure 4-18.) This moves the fulcrum to its leftmost position.

◎ Now, pull the ball release lever.

Fig. 4-18. Adjust the console pegs as shown to move the fulcrum to its leftmost position.

If you've done it correctly, another ice sphere rolls out of the Central Tower and clips the multicolored ball, sending it into the Balance Bridge catch-basket to balance the bridge just before the ice sphere reaches it. The ice sphere crosses safely this time and returns to the tower.

At the same time, the console casing folds in, showing a bridge being raised near the offshore platform. Then the casing closes in on itself again, this time locking into place. A hexagonal code is etched on the casing—one of three such codes necessary to complete the Central Tower walkway.

Fig. 4-19. Here's the hexagonal code revealed on the console for the Balance Bridge.

◎ Sketch the code. (Or better yet, just put a bookmark in this page for later reference to figure 4-19.) Note that this symbol's border is yellow. It will be important later on.

◎ Return to the basalt cavern via the wooden walkway.

◎ When you reach the fork in the tunnel, go left and proceed past the elevator.

◎ Continue down the remarkable tunnel lit by more of those oddly glowing blue crystals.

◎ When you emerge from the tunnel, approach the set of rungs carved into a column on your right.

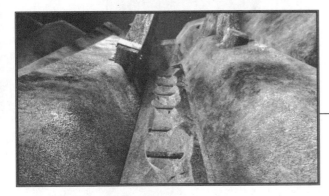

Fig. 4-20. Climb these rungs carved in the basalt column to find the Resonance Ring Puzzle control panel.

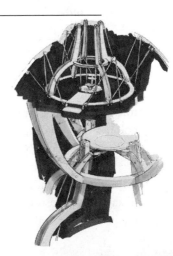

◎ Climb the rungs.

◎ At the top, walk down the wooden track leading to the Central Tower. When the track ends abruptly over water, turn left to see a walkway.

◎ Follow the walkway to a platform with another control panel: the Resonance Ring Puzzle console.

The Resonance Ring Puzzle

The Resonance Ring Puzzle is a looping, roller-coaster-like section of track with a special Amateria twist. Note the roofed ring structures at the end of each loop or "arm" of the track circuit. A column tipped by a glowing blue crystal towers above each ring. Each crystal generates one of five harmonic frequencies that vibrate the air within the resonance ring below, forming a rippling barrier of sound waves.

Fig. 4-21. The Resonance Ring Puzzle tracks curve and loop through five resonance rings. Towering blue crystals generate the rings.

Control Panel

- Approach the control panel and turn right. Saavedro left another set of journal pages on one end of the cross-shaped platform.

- Pick up the pages and read them.

Saavedro writes of the first visit to Narayan of Sirrus and Achenar, as boys. But in his fevered mind he melds this meeting with other, future events that occurred when the boys had returned as young men with "something dark…in their eyes."

- Step up to the control panel.

- Turn left and pull the long-handled lever at left to raise the platform. This gives you a stunning view of not only the Resonance Ring Puzzle tracks, but also the other structures around the island.

◎ Examine the control panel. Note the buttons and their corresponding odd-shaped gears. Take special note of the order of the gears.

◎ Pull the console lever (just left of the gears) and watch the amazing result.

Fig. 4-22. Cool!

Wow! The cupola-like top of the Central Tower levitates into the air! Even more amazing, it seems to spawn an ice sphere out of thin air. The sphere then drops onto the track and rolls toward the crisscrossing, five-armed set of tracks down below. But suddenly, on the first loop, it shatters.

Why? Because it hit the barrier within an active resonance ring. We'll examine the resonance rings up close in a moment.

◎ Pull the handle again.

◎ After the tower top levitates and deposits another sphere on the track, watch the control panel.

How the Timer Works

The Resonance Ring Puzzle control panel is a timing mechanism. When activated, it shuttles a ball bearing through five gears; as the bearing rolls, it depresses five blue buttons in sequence. Each button, when pressed, turns off all resonance rings set to a particular frequency. Again, each button is paired with one of the odd-shaped gears. Thus, each gear is associated with a particular frequency. This becomes important in a moment.

As mentioned earlier, each blue crystal out on the Resonance Ring Puzzle can generate one of five frequencies. As you might expect, the five frequencies that can be generated by the crystals are the same five turned off by the blue console buttons. When a button is pressed, *any* crystal generating that particular frequency is disabled; it flicks off as long as the ball bearing depresses the button.

Again, each blue crystal generates the sound barrier in the resonance ring just below it. So when a button deactivates a crystal, it also deactivates the crystal's resonance ring.

Fig. 4-23. Watch the ball bearing move around the panel, depressing buttons as it goes.

So here's the trick. Each blue crystal on the Resonance Ping Puzzle can be set *manually* to one of the five frequencies controlled by the console buttons. If you walk the tracks, following the path the ice sphere would roll, you can set the crystal frequencies to the same order as the console buttons. Then, as the ice sphere rolls through the Resonance Ring Puzzle, the ball bearing simultaneously rolls over the buttons, turning off each resonance ring just before the ice sphere reaches it.

Whew! Got it? If not, don't worry. It will make more sense as we walk through the solution steps below.

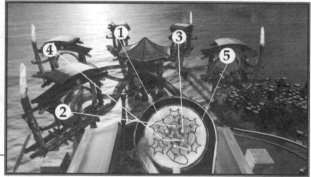

Fig. 4-24. Each blue console button, when pressed, toggles off a frequency. Use the odd gear shapes to match the crystal frequencies out on the loops to the order of the buttons (as shown here).

- ◎ Pull the tall lever at far left to lower the platform to the ground.
- ◎ Head back down the track to the ladder.
- ◎ Descend the ladder, turn right, and enter the watery cave just ahead.

Saavedro's Cave

◎ Check out Saavedro's mural on the wall. Monstrous, laughing images of Sirrus and Achenar float above a pitched battle. In the middle of the conflict stands a man—Saavedro, no doubt.

Fig. 4-25. Saavedro's mural depicts the Narayan civil war.

◎ Follow the wooden walkway out of the cave. Ahead you see a series of curved, crumbling basalt columns; it looks like the skeleton of a whale.

◎ Scramble over fallen chunks of basalt until you reach the Resonance Ring Puzzle tracks.

◎ Climb up onto the tracks and turn left.

Setting the Resonance Rings

With the Central Tower behind you and the looping arms of the track ahead of you, it's time to think like an ice sphere; that is, follow the path a rolling sphere would take. At the tip of each track loop, you find a resonance ring and its frequency control dial.

Fig. 4-26. Here's where you start your trek across the Resonance Ring Puzzle track loops, adjusting the crystal frequencies as you go.

◎ Walk *straight* through the small pagoda-covered intersection. Don't veer off onto one of the crossing tracks under the pagoda!

◎ Follow the track out onto the arm loop.

Soon you hear the resonating hum of the first resonance ring, and you see the ripple of its clear concentric vibrations. These sonic vibrations cause the ice sphere to shatter when it attempts to pass through them. You, however, can walk right through it if you want.

◎ Don't walk through the ring yet. Instead, walk past the ring down the ramp extending to a small dial on a post.

◎ Zoom in on the dial for a close up.

Fig. 4-27. Walk down the ramp beyond each ring and set the dial pointer to the correct frequency. Here's the setting for the first dial.

The dial has a pointer that you can move to five different positions. Odd gear shapes that match those from the Resonance Ring Puzzle's control panel mark the five positions. Each pointer position sets a different frequency for the crystal (and hence, for the crystal's resonance ring). You can hear the difference when you move the pointer.

Again, each frequency is marked by a gear shape; that particular frequency is disabled by the console button framed by the same gear shape. Here, the gear shape in the upper left (10 o'clock) position is the same as the first gear shape in the ball bearing sequence.

◎ Click on the gear at the 10 o'clock position to move the pointer there. (See figure 4-27.) As you do, the crystal's frequency changes.

◎ Walk back to the ring and then duck through it. For a second, as you stand within the ring itself, the camera shakes.

◎ Follow the curve of the track downward through the lower tunnel in the pagoda, another four-way intersection. Again, where would the ball roll? Veer slightly right (not a hard right) and head up to the curve of the next arm.

- Step into the resonance ring. You should see the Central Tower vibrating madly in front of you.

- Turn right and step onto the ramp to the frequency dial. You should see the collapsing "whale-bone" basalt columns to your left. (See figure 4-28.)

Fig. 4-28. Here's the view from the ramp off the second resonance ring.

Fig. 4-29. Set the second ring's dial to the 12 o'clock position.

- Again, zoom in to the dial for a close-up.

- Click on the gear shape at the very top (it matches the gear associated with the second console button) to set the pointer to the 12 o'clock position. Once again, you'll hear a change in the ring's resonating sound.

- Return to the track. Follow it upward and straight through the pagoda intersection to the third arm.

- Again, step out onto the ramp. Across the water behind the dial you should see dozens of hexagonal pools.

- Zoom in on the dial and set this pointer to the 2 o'clock position.

Fig. 4-30. Here's the view of the third ring's dial. Set it to the 2 o'clock position as shown here.

- Walk to the left through the third resonance ring and head down to the lower track intersection.
- After you enter the intersection, pivot slightly to the right and go through the middle of the three openings to proceed to the fourth resonance ring.
- Step through the ring and follow the ramp to the dial.
- Set this dial's pointer to the 4 o'clock position.

Fig. 4-31. Here's the view from the fourth ring's ramp. Set the dial to the 4 o'clock position as shown here.

◎ Now follow the track heading upward and straight through the pagoda to the fifth and final ring.

◎ Follow the ramp to the dial. You should be looking directly down at the hexagonal pools, with the Turntable Tracks structure visible in the near distance.

◎ Set the dial pointer to the 6 o'clock position.

Fig. 4-32. Here's the view from the fifth ring's dial ramp. Set the dial to the 6 o'clock position as shown here.

At this point, all of the resonance ring frequencies should be aligned to match the frequencies being turned off by the Resonance Ring Puzzle control panel as the ball bearing makes its circuit through the gears. But there's only one sure way to check.

◎ Step back onto the track, pivot slightly right, and follow it upward to the pagoda intersection.

◎ In the intersection, turn left so you're facing the Central Tower.

◎ Walk toward the tower until the track ends, then scramble back down over the collapsed columns to Saavedro's cave.

◎ Make your way around the perimeter of the cave, and then proceed up the carved rung ladder to the Resonance Ring Puzzle control panel.

◎ Turn left and pull the long handle to raise the platform.

◎ Pull the console lever to release another sphere.

The tower top levitates again, and another crystal sphere materializes and drops onto the track. With all the rings working correctly, the sphere makes it through the circuit without exploding, and returns back to the tower safely. Well done!

Now watch the console casing fold in, showing another bridge being raised near the offshore structure. Then the casing closes in on itself, this time locking into place. A hexagonal code is etched on the casing—the second of three such codes necessary to complete the Central Tower walkway.

Fig. 4-33. Here's your reward for successful completion of the Resonance Ring Puzzle.

- ◎ Sketch this code for later. (Or better yet, jot down "figure 4-33" for later reference.) Note that the symbol's border is blue. It will be important later on.

- ◎ Retrace your route through the mural cavern and back to the Resonance Ring Puzzle tracks.

- ◎ After you climb onto the tracks, walk to the pagoda intersection and turn hard right. This puts you onto the track that runs back down to the fifth resonance ring.

- ◎ Follow the track through the resonance ring and over the hexagonal pools. Continue until the wood slats abruptly end.

- ◎ Pivot left and step onto the moss-covered columns.

- ◎ Follow this path until you find a slatted door on your left.

- ◎ Go through the slatted door and approach the Turntable Tracks control panel.

Turntable Tracks

Fig. 4-34. The Turntable Tracks loom ahead.

The Turntable Tracks structure features four track arches curving between two large, rotating wheels. Each wheel has six rings; half of these rings are open, and the other half hold powerful spring mechanisms. Your task is to set the control panel so that an ice sphere from the Central Tower works its way (via wheel rotation and spring action) back and forth between the wheels. The sphere must end up in an open ring at the right-hand wheel's top-left position (see position 4 in figure 4-37) to return to the Central Tower.

Control Panel

- After you step through the slatted door, turn right and look down. Saavedro left another journal page sitting on a mossy rock.

- Read the pages. Saavedro writes again of the trickery and false promises of Sirrus and Achenar.

Fig. 4-35. Don't miss these journal pages just inside the gate to the Turntable Tracks control platform.

◎ Step up to the Turntable Tracks controls.

◎ Pull the long-handled lever and watch as your platform rises into the air.

◎ Examine the control panel. You see two dials and, in a tray below, three pegs.

Experiment with the pegs; pop them into holes and pull the lever to see what happens. Note that when the ice sphere sits on the left wheel, the wheel and the control panel's left dial turn counterclockwise. When the ice sphere sits on the right wheel, that wheel and the control panel's right dial turn clockwise. Whenever a peg rotates to the bottom position of a control panel dial, it slides through a hole and drops back into the tray, and the ice sphere on the wheel below is launched.

Recall that four sets of arched tracks guide the ice sphere from wheel to wheel. If the sphere is not aligned with one of these sets of tracks when its wheel stops turning, it shatters. If the sphere lands in a ring without a spring, it falls through and shatters.

With a little analysis and experimentation, you can plan a course for the ice sphere that moves it to where you desire. See the broken peg opening? More sabotage. Originally, Atrus designed several ways to solve this puzzle, but Saavedro wants you to do it the hard way.

Stumped? Read on for the answer:

◎ Place pegs in the holes located at the 12 and 2 o'clock positions on the left dial. Place the remaining peg in the hole located at the 10 o'clock position on the left dial. (See figure 4-36.)

◎ Pull the lever to release the ice sphere from the Central Tower.

Fig. 4-36. Put the pegs in these holes and pull the release lever to solve the puzzle.

Here's what happens. All numbers refer to those called out in figure 4-37:

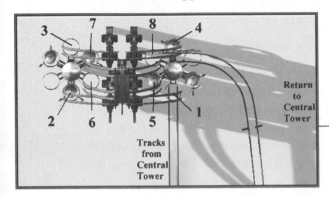

Fig. 4-37. Overhead view of the Turntable Tracks.

- ◎ The ice sphere arrives at 1 and shoots over to a spring-filled ring at 2.

- ◎ The left wheel rotates counterclockwise three positions until the peg you placed at 12 o'clock halts the rotation; the ice sphere is now at 3.

- ◎ The spring shoots the sphere over to a spring-filled ring at 4.

- ◎ The right wheel rotates clockwise four positions until the peg you placed at 10 o'clock halts the rotation; the ice sphere is now at 5.

- ◎ The spring shoots the sphere over to a spring-filled ring at 6.

- ◎ The left wheel rotates counterclockwise one position until the peg you placed at 2 o'clock halts the rotation; the ice sphere is now at 7.

- ◎ The spring shoots the sphere over to an open ring at 8, which allows the sphere to drop through and roll down the return track to the Central Tower.

The console casing folds in, showing the last bridge being raised near the offshore platform. Then the casing closes in on itself, locking into place. A hexagonal code is etched on the casing—the third of the three codes necessary to complete the Central Tower walkway.

Fig. 4-38. Here's the hexagonal code revealed when you solve the Turntable Tracks Puzzle.

◎ Note that the symbol's border is green. It will be important later.

◎ Pull the lever to lower the platform.

◎ Go through the slatted gate and turn left.

◎ Follow the path all the way back to the pagoda where you first arrived in Amateria—the one with the incomplete walkway to the Central Tower.

Tower Entry: The Hexagon Codes

◎ Step up the walkway toward the tower and turn left to face the podium with the hexagonal buttons.

◎ Click on the podium and enter any of the three codes from the control panels (Turntable Tracks, Balance Bridge, or the Resonance Ring Puzzle).

◎ Click to zoom away. Two bridge flaps rise to span the first gap in the walkway.

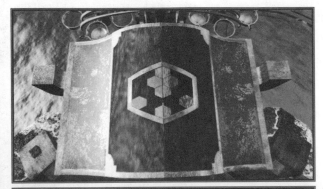

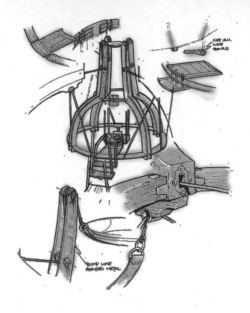

Fig. 4-39. For the sake of convenience, here again are the three hexagon codes you discovered at the three perimeter structures.

- Repeat this at the next two podiums, entering the other two hexagon codes to complete the walkway to the Central Tower.

- Open the door and enter the tower.

Note: The podium codes will not work until the structure it corresponds to is correctly set. A mechanism in the bridge checks this to keep explorers in the age safe. You'll see why later

Tower Interior

The tower interior is divided into two sections: the switchyard base and the circular top floor. As its name implies, the base contains an immense, track-covered switchyard. Tracks curve up, down, and around in total disarray across nine circular platforms.

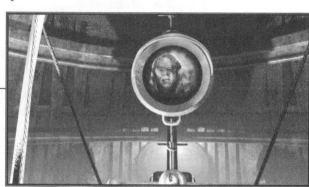

Fig. 4-40. Climb the stairs to the imager for another message from Saavedro.

◎ When you first step into the tower, a precarious stairway swings into place. Climb it to the chair in the middle of the tower. Note the imager installed behind the chair.

◎ Click on the chair to spin it around.

◎ Step forward to sit in the chair. Then push the botton to activate the message from Saavedro.

◎ When the imager message ends, a control handle will rotate down from above you. Pull the handle to raise the chair above the tower.

From this position, you can see the entire island. Looking above you, you can see four colored buttons that launch ice spheres toward the different structures on the map. But you hear each sphere get destroyed when it re-enters the pagoda. Perhaps the tracks below you aren't correctly aligned.

Fig. 4-41. Four colored buttons above your head launch ice spheres out to Amateria's structures: green to the Turntable Tracks, blue to the Resonance Ring Puzzle, yellow to the Balance Bridge, and red to the offshore structure.

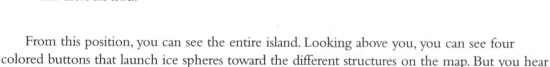

○ Look at the colored buttons above you. Here's how the colors correspond to the structures outside:

green = Turntable Tracks

blue = Resonance Ring Puzzle

yellow = Balance Bridge

red = Offshore structure

○ If you recall, these are also the colors that bordered the panels with the hexagonal codes after you solved each of these puzzles.

○ Approach the wooden control console; this controls the tracks below. Perhaps you can arrange the tracks in a pattern that an ice sphere can roll through.

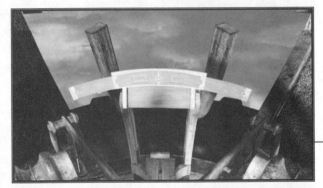

○ Click on the console for a close-up of the switchyard controls (see figure 4-42).

Fig. 4-42. This control console controls the tracks in the switchyard below.

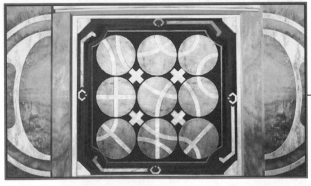

Fig. 4-43. Here's what the switchyard puzzle looks like when you first reach it.

See the colored paths that curve around the corners? The colors correspond to the same structures as do the buttons above; these paths show you where the ice sphere exits and enters the Central Tower as it travels through the respective structures around the island. Your ultimate goal is to roll a sphere to the entrance of the red path at the very top of the console—that is, to the offshore structure.

Of course, the three final segments of track leading to that offshore structure are still in the water. But remember how you saw a scene of each track segment rising out of the water when you solved each of the three puzzles around the island? It makes sense that by sending the ball through all three of Amateria's structures (Turntable Tracks, Balance Bridge, and Resonance Ring Puzzle) before you direct it to the offshore structure, you can raise all three bridge segments first.

◎ Examine the console. For clarity's sake, let's number the segments of the switchyard controls:

◎ Note also that the C-shaped "entrances" of the colored segments (marking where ice spheres from the Central Tower enter each Amateria structure) sit at the four compass points on the console. At the other end of each colored segment is an "exit" (where the sphere returns into the tower).

Switchyard Puzzle Solution

◎ In general, start with segment 2 and build a path backward from the entrance of the offshore structure's red path (your final target) to the exit of another colored path.

◎ Click segment 2 one time to create a path to segment 6.

◎ Follow the path through segment 6 to segment 9. Click 9 one time to create a path to 8.

◎ Click 8 one time to create a path to 7.

◎ Click 7 one time to arrange a path through 4 and 1 to the exit of the green segment. Phew! At this point, your console switches should be arranged as in figure 4-44.

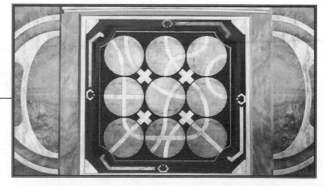

Fig. 4-44. Here's the switchyard puzzle at the halfway point.

◎ Following the path from the green segment's entrance, click 5 twice to open a path to the exit of the yellow segment.

◎ Click 3 one time to complete a path to the exit of the blue segment. Voilà! When you're done, your masterpiece looks like figure 4-45.

◎ With the tracks arranged, press the blue button to send an ice sphere rolling out toward the Resonance Rings.

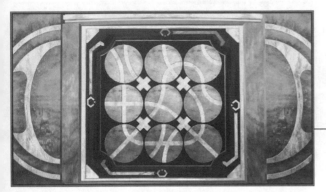

Fig. 4-45. Set the switchyard controls to this final configuration. Now a sphere can roll unhindered from blue to yellow to green to red.

An ice sphere launched from the Central Tower rolls out toward the "blue" structure, the Resonance Rings, returns to the tower, raises one segment of track to the offshore structure, and then heads for the "yellow" structure, the Balance Bridge. When the sphere crosses the fulcrum bridge and returns to the tower again, the second segment of track to the offshore structure rises. Next the sphere rolls out to the "green" structure, Turntable Tracks, and then back through the tower, raising the third segment of track. Finally, the sphere heads off to the "red" offshore structure.

After the ice sphere successfully navigates the entire Amateria circuit, a new sphere forms around you and your chair and then rolls through the massive track you just created. Your joyride ends at the offshore structure. As you roll into your final position, the Amateria symbol slides into view. Automatically, you sketch it on a page from your journal.

◎ Approach the J'nanin linking book.

◎ Use the book to return to the Observatory.

Back to J'nanin

When you return to J'nanin from Amateria with the Dynamic Forces symbol, you link directly into the second floor of the Observatory.

- ◎ Approach the imaging table.

- ◎ Take your sketch of the Dynamic Forces symbol from inventory and put it on the imaging table.

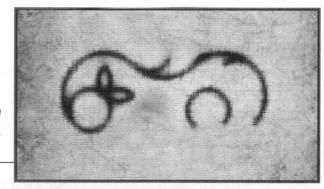

Fig. 4-46. Take the Dynamic Forces symbol sketch from inventory and place it on the imaging table.

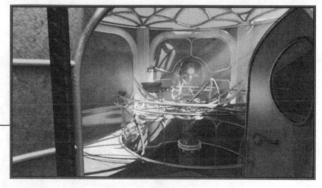

Fig. 4-47. The cams rotate, opening the book cage. But you still can't reach it.

The imager projects the sketch downward, raising a 3-D representation of the symbol from a cam beneath the table. Another cam drops down, imprinting the 3-D symbol on its elastic surface. Then the cams rotate, manipulating the cage mechanism.

If you're following this walkthrough, Amateria is the second Element Age you visit. Thus, placing the symbol sketch on the imaging table opens the cage in the pit. Another hologram projector message from Saavedro plays on the ceiling. (See the Note here.) This second message hints at Saavedro's misunderstanding of the Art of writing Ages.

"I read all about the D'ni," he says. "How you started their world again. Can you really do that, Atrus? After everything that's happened to Narayan, could you start the world over again?"

Note: Remember you can bring back symbols from the Ages *in any order*. When placed on the imaging table, each symbol activates some aspect of the cage mechanism in the pit, then triggers a hologram message from Saavedro. Whether from Voltaic, Amateria, or Edanna, the first symbol placed on the imaging table raises the cage from the pit, the second symbol opens the cage, and the third symbol extends a ramp to the cage. Saavedro's messages play in the same order regardless of the order in which you solve the Ages.

◎ Once you bring back a second Age symbol and use it on the imaging table, the blue button thereafter triggers the same message ("This what you expected, Atrus?") until another Age symbol is retrieved and placed on the table.

◎ Go to the doors and exit the Observatory onto the high bridge.

◎ Solve the next linking book puzzle. In this walkthrough, we'll go to Edanna next. See "Getting from J'nanin to Edanna" in Chapter 2, J'nanin: The Lesson Age.

Chapter 5
Edanna
The Nature Age

Prima's Official Strategy Guide

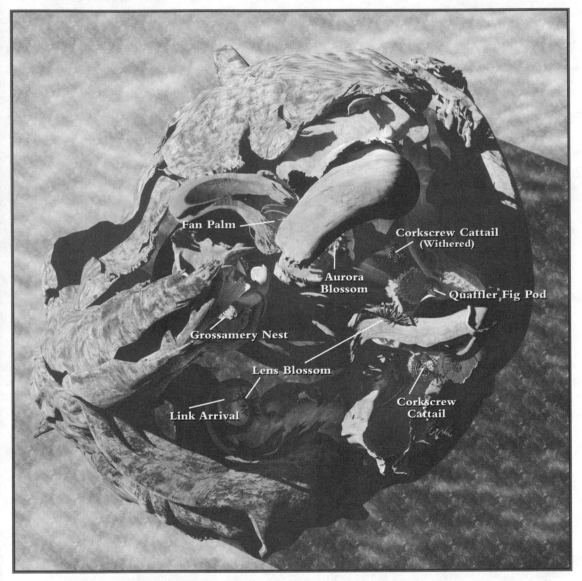

Fan Palm

Corkscrew Cattail
(Withered)

Aurora
Blossom

Quaffler Fig Pod

Grossamery Nest

Lens Blossom

Corkscrew
Cattail

Link Arrival

Fig. 5-1. Here's an overhead view of Deadwood Ridge, the upper level of Edanna.

primagames.com

Edanna is a fantastic, living edifice that rises some 200 feet above the ocean. Your fly-by approach (see figure 5-2) reveals its tree-like structure. Unlike most trees, however, Edanna grows *inward*. Knotted, sun-bleached branches weave a labyrinth down the trunk's interior, creating three distinct ecosystems: the dry Deadwood Ridge at the top; the lush, canopied forest in the middle; and finally, the murky, saltwater swamp at the base.

Your primary goal in Edanna, as in the other Ages, is to find its unique symbol. To do so, you must first discover how various plants and animals in the Age react to different stimuli: light, touch, the presence of symbiotic and predatory plants and creatures, and so on. As you explore, remember the enlightened observation in Atrus' journal: "Nature encourages mutual dependence."

> **Note:** Your ultimate goal in each of the three Element Ages is the same: find the Age's unique symbol, then bring it back to J'nanin.

Fig. 5-2. Your approach to Edanna reveals its vertical, inward structure.

Deadwood Ridge

You arrive on a stark, well-lit ridge formed by Edanna's abrupt decision to grow inward. Deadwood Ridge features three separate levels: upper, middle, and lower. You arrive in the middle level. Branches curve and wend their way downward from here, forming ledges and walkways along the great trunk's inner walls. Huge, buttercup-like blossoms collect rainwater. Near these petal-held pools rise giant Corkscrew Cattails. Other unusual plants sprout nearby to form a symbiotic ecosystem.

Arrival: Middle Ridge

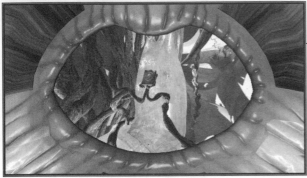

Fig. 5-3. The tangled vines at left house a useful object. Use the nearby Lens Blossom to spot it—a J'nanin linking book!

❥ You arrive next to a tangle of vines. Inside the tangle, dripping sap has hardened to amber. And...say, is that a book in there?

❥ Step behind the petals of the flowering plant just right of the vines. This is a Lens Blossom.

❥ Look through the Lens Blossom to see the J'nanin linking book delicately supported by a pair of vines. Bizarre!

❥ Turn around and follow the path to a Corkscrew Cattail, the tall, spiraling plant.

❥ Step onto the cattail and let its rippling spiral leaf whisk you to the top of the ridge.

Fig. 5-4. Climb this Corkscrew Cattail to the top of Deadwood Ridge.

Upper Ridge

At the top, look to the left of the Corkscrew Cattail. Its tendril draws water from a nearby basin formed by the flowering top of a vine plant called a Quaffler Fig. (More on that later.) It seems the big cattail needs constant hydration.

Fig. 5-5. Note the symbiosis: the Corkscrew Cattail's tendril drinks from a natural pool formed in the Quaffler Fig's flowering top.

- Turn and climb the slope. Suddenly, a giant bird carrying a succulent pod swoops into a nearby nest. Say, isn't that a Redbreasted Grossamery?

- Continue up the slope to the Lens Blossom.

Built into the curving sweep of a broken branch at the center of the ridge, the Grossamery nest contains eggshells and a newly arrived hatchling. Below the nest, the J'nanin linking book lies half-hidden and inaccessible within its sap-covered tangle of vines.

Fig. 5-6. The bird nest perches directly atop the natural chamber of vines that holds the J'nanin linking book.

Fig. 5-7. Here's the close-up view of the nest as seen through the Lens Blossom.

❤ Look through the Lens Blossom. The mother Grossamery feeds succulents to her newborn chick. Cool!

❤ Return down the slope toward the Corkscrew Cattail and then turn left. See the ocean through the circular gap in the trunk?

❤ Walk through the gap.

❤ Continue down the path to the bulbous, fluid-filled pod sprouting from a vine. As you reach it, the mother bird exits the nest in search of more food for her chick.

❤ Touch the pod to see its inner fluids ripple. Awesome!

Fig. 5-8. The drinking tendril of a withered Corkscrew Cattail seeks water in the bone-dry basin of a Quaffler Fig's flowering top. A water-filled fig pod hangs nearby.

This pod is actually part of the Quaffler Fig plant. Indeed, the Quaffler Fig is a "plant system" that includes a flower basin that gathers rainwater on top and a hollow, tube-like vine extending beneath that sprouts one or more fig pods. These huge pods can suck water down through the fig's vine from the flower basin. The pod here, for example, is fully laden with water.

Note a few other things about this location (see figure 5–8). First, the water-filled fig pod hangs from its vine over a dry basin. To the right, another Corkscrew Cattail shoots up from below. This one, however, is withered and retracted, so you can't walk down its spiral leaf. The cattail's drinking tendril reaches to the dry, empty basin in a fruitless search for water.

- Continue up the slope, following the path all the way to the top. At left, an Aurora Blossom sits in the shade of a Fan Palm to the right.

- Approach the Aurora Blossom. Its petals curl over an inner lens formed of hardened sap.

- Touch the blossom's stamen to open the petals, and then look through the lens.

Fig. 5-9. An Aurora Blossom sits in the shade of a Fan Palm. Move the palm to shed a little light.

The lens views the plants you just passed below: the Quaffler Fig pod, the flower basin of a second fig, and the Corkscrew Cattail. See that black, charred mark on the branch just right of the water-filled pod? Looks like something burned the tree.

- Turn around and approach the Fan Palm.

- Press the heart of the Fan Palm. Its fronds respond by stretching skyward, revealing another J'nanin linking book.

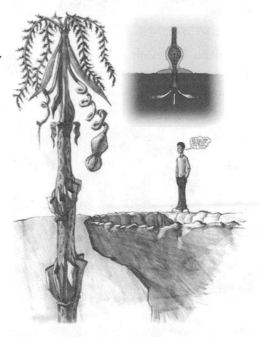

This is a safety-valve book; it sends you back to the Edanna book chamber. You won't need it if you follow our golden path. More important, the Fan Palm's rise means its fronds no longer shade the Aurora Blossom.

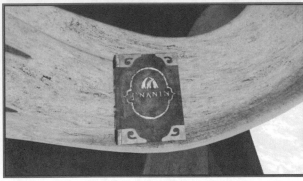

Fig. 5-10. Press the Fan Palm heart to raise the fronds, revealing a J'nanin linking book and letting the sun shine on the Aurora Blossom.

- Go back to the big flower, open the petals, and look through the lens again.

- See the hot spot? The Aurora Blossom's lens channels the sunlight into a burning focus, much like a magnifying glass.

- Aim the hotspot at the Quaffler Fig pod.

After a few seconds, the pod bursts, spilling its contents into the flower basin below. Immediately, the Corkscrew Cattail's tendril begins sucking up the precious fluid, hydrating the big plant, which in turn unfurls its spiral leaf the length of the stalk.

Fig. 5-11. After the pod bursts, the tendril drinks from the basin, hydrating the cattail's spiral leaf.

- Head back down the path to the newly hydrated Corkscrew Cattail, now unfurled and ready.
- Climb down the vine.

Lower Ridge: The Swing Vine

Fig. 5-12. Here's a cutaway view from overhead of the lower ridge where you encounter the swing vine puzzle.

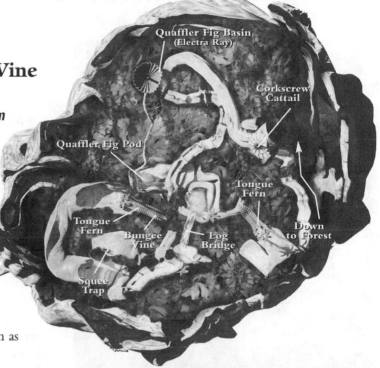

On the lower level of Deadwood Ridge, the great tree-island's inward-growing branches become a twisted maze of shadowy walking paths and dead ends. This area is not as lush as the densely canopied forest below; in fact, its center forms a sheer, open drop into the canopy, but neither is it as stark and barren as the ridge levels above.

Fig. 5-13. An Electra Ray patrols the flower basin. Note how the fish electrifies the plant roots it feeds on.

- From the bottom of the cattail, walk down the path formed by the tree's interweaving branches past a stand of low palms to another basin formed by the flowering top of a Quaffler Fig.
- Watch the Electra Ray as it shocks the underwater roots of a plant and feeds off of it.
- Step to the left side of the pool and note the long, tubelike stem underneath.
- Continue walking down the path, lit spectacularly by glowing lavender lichen. You eventually reach a spiky pod on your right.

This is a fig pod, unfilled. Note that the pod is attached to the same tubelike vine that runs from the basin above. Again, the pod, the vine, and the basin are all parts of the same Quaffler Fig plant.

Fig. 5-14. When you touch the spiky fig pod, it expands, sucking water and the Electra Ray through the tube stem from the basin above.

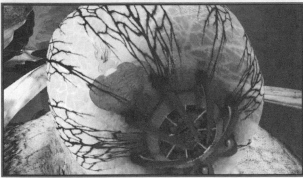

♥ Do you dare touch this thing? Of course you do! Watch it expand, sucking water *and* the Electra Ray down through the tube from the basin. Now it looks like the pod you burst earlier, but adds the translucent red of the fish's glow.

♥ Turn around. You see the lavender-lit passage you just came down at left, and a yellow-lit passage to the right. Step toward the yellow lit passage to find another set of Saavedro's journal entries on the ground.

♥ Enter the yellow-lit passage.

♥ You emerge from the passage to see a perilous drop just ahead. To your right, a log, rotted and covered with Barnacle Moss, spans the drop. It seems deliberately placed as a bridge.

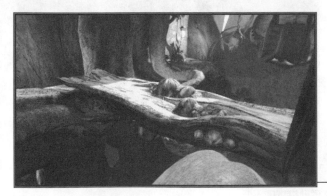

Fig. 5-15. This log serves first as a convenient bridge, then later as an inconvenient impediment blocking your swing route.

- Cross the rotted log and follow the tunnel-like path (speckled with purple dots of glowing lichen) as it curves right. You come to a tightly curled Tongue Fern.

- Pull the coil on the fern's lanternlike symbiotic spore. The spore opens, emitting light that stimulates the fern to unfurl.

- Take one step out onto the Tongue Fern.

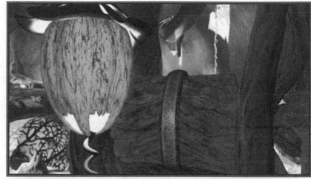

Fig. 5-16. Pull the spore's coil to shine light on the Tongue Fern. The light causes the fern to unfurl.

Now have a good look around. Straight ahead, the rotten log spans the gap. A swinglike handle on a vine hangs over the tip of the Tongue Fern. To your immediate left you see the reddish glow of the fig pod with the Electra Ray. Off to the right, a small tentlike structure is rigged to a rope; it looks like a trap, with its rope running to a handle wrapped around a branch right next to you. Note also the pink fruit growing on vines near the trap.

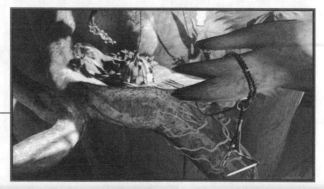

Fig. 5-17. Is that a trap across the gap? Its rope runs to the handle attached to a nearby branch.

- Walk to the end of the unfurled Tongue Fern.

- Look up and click on the swing handle to pull it down.

- Click on the rotten log to take a swing in that direction. Fun!

Fig. 5-18. Pull down that vine swing. It swings in two different directions, but the rotten log blocks one way.

Problem, though. As you swing under the rotten log, you see a promising ledge on the far side. But the rotten log blocks the way; the vine hits it, whipping the swing right back to the Tongue Fern each time. So your next task is to eliminate the log, thus opening up the swing path to that far ledge.

- Turn right and click on the ledge with the trap. This time you swing across and land cleanly right next to the trap, facing a crank handle.

- Approach the handle and give it a crank! This raises the trap.

- Step toward the raised trap and shake a pink fruit loose from the vine behind it.

- Important! Click on the loose piece of fruit to roll it out from underneath the trap.

Fig. 5-19. After you raise the trap, knock down a fruit, and then push the fruit out from underneath the trap.

This last step may seem strange, but here's why you do it: You want to get rid of the rotten log so you can swing to the far ledge. The log, remember, is encrusted with Barnacle Moss. Do you recall what happens to that plant when a Squee chirps? The moss buds expand to twice their original size. And there just happens to be a Squee's nest nearby. So your task is to lure or chase a chirping Squee toward the rotten log.

Fig. 5-20. When you leave the trap area, the Squee sneaks out to munch the fruit bait.

But if you actually trap the Squee (which you can do if you leave the fruit where it originally falls), the creature stays in the trap until you raise it with the crank handle. Then the Squee simply runs back into his nest. So your goal is to lure the Squee *away from* the hanging trap, then drop the trap to block the path into its nest. The Squee will run toward the rotten, moss-encrusted log.

- After you move the fruit out from under the trap, head into the passage behind the crank handle. This slides you down a one-way ramp.

- At the bottom of the ramp, turn right and retrace your route through the tunnel to the Tongue Fern.

- Take one step onto the fern. You automatically turn to see the Squee exit his nest and munch happily on the fruit offering.

- Pull the trap's release handle on the branch just to your right.

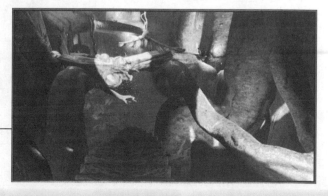

Fig. 5-21. Pull the handle by the Tongue Fern to drop the trap. The Squee hops to the log, chirps to expand the Barnacle Moss buds, and down it goes!

The trap falls, blocking the Squee's route back into its nest. It hesitates a moment, then makes a beeline for the rotten log. When the creature sees its favorite food growing there, it chirps to reach the delicate flowers and nectar within. The Barnacle Moss expands, the rotting wood gives way, and the bridge breaks apart, clearing the path for your daredevil swing.

- ❤ Step to the end of the Tongue Fern and pull down the swing handle again.

- ❤ Click in that direction to make the vine swing to the other side. You land in front of a previously inaccessible tunnel.

- ❤ Once across, approach the Tongue Fern and pull the coil on its symbiotic spore. The spore glows brightly, unfurling the fern to form a bridge across the gap. Now you have a route back to the upper levels of Deadwood Ridge, should you need one.

- ❤ Proceed down the lichen-lit path to the right of the Tongue Fern.

Edanna Forest

Edanna's dense forest is a true botanical wonder. Some of the flora is familiar by now: Tongue Ferns, Aurora Blossoms, and a further extension of the Quaffler Fig vine from above. But down here a pearlescent, orchidlike flower with reflective qualities makes its first appearance, as does one of Saavedro's specially bred predatory growths.

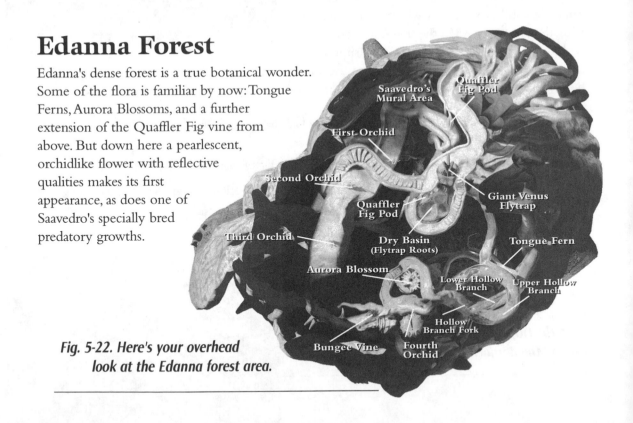

Fig. 5-22. Here's your overhead look at the Edanna forest area.

Fig. 5-23. Uh oh! The mother Grossamery is trapped in the Venus flytrap.

❧ Follow the undulating path down into the forest.

❧ Stop and examine the giant Venus flytrap.

The poor mother Grossamery is trapped inside the carnivorous plant! How can we get it out? Think back to your exploration of Saavedro's living quarters on the first floor of the J'nanin Observatory. Remember the smaller flytrap on his work desk? When you zapped its roots with electricity, the trap opened. You can do the same to this larger version. But where can we find a source of electricity in Edanna?

❧ First, examine the flytrap's long spindly roots. They thread downward. Let's find out where they end up.

❧ Turn around and spot the path leading outside Edanna's trunk through a narrow opening (just left of the path you came down. See figure 5-24.) overhung with vines.

Fig. 5-24. From the trapped bird, find this opening that leads outside the great trunk.

❧ Follow this new path to a ledge overlooking the ocean.

❧ Turn left and take the yellow-lit path. Notice the Quaffler Fig vine dropping down from above and running along the path.

❧ Follow the path until you reach another spiky fig pod sitting beneath a painted mural.

Fig. 5-25. Another Quaffler Fig pod rests beneath an elaborate "message" mural painted by Saavedro.

The mural is another message to Atrus from Saavedro, and it's not hard to decipher. Sirrus and Achenar speak to enthralled young people while worried elders listen nearby. The brothers hold up books (Age linking books, no doubt), which recalls Saavedro's hologram message after you returned to J'nanin with the first symbol: "All that talk about fixing instabilities, rewriting the Age so that we would be free to live our lives…that was just talk to hide the truth of why they had come." (Note: If Edanna is your first Age visit, you haven't seen Saavedro's hologram message yet.)

The fig pod, by the way, is attached to the vine dropping from above. Could this be part of the same Quaffler Fig plant system we manipulated earlier? Let's find out.

💜 Touch the pod. Sure enough, it sucks water and the Electra Ray down the vine from the previous pod. (This works only if you've previously sucked the fish from the original basin to the fig pod just above the vine.) Note also how the vine continues on downward from this now-swollen pod. More pods below?

💜 Find the thorny roots of the Venus flytrap just to the left of the mural. Take a step toward them.

💜 When you reach the roots, you can see two paths. Take the left path.

Fig. 5-26. The Quaffler Fig's vine (lower right) and the Venus flytrap's thorny roots (straight ahead) appear to converge and then drop together.

🦋 Descend the crude stairs and follow the path as it curves around to yet another Quaffler Fig pod. Its vine drops down from above. Could it be part of the same vine system through which we've been shuttling the Electra Ray?

🦋 Touch the pod. Yes, here comes the poor fish.

🦋 Note that this swollen pod hangs over an empty basin, and one bundle of the Venus flytrap's thorny roots wind through that same basin. Any ideas?

Fig. 5-27. Suck the Electra Ray down into the fig pod that dangles over a basin where the Venus flytrap roots run.

Yes, you got it. Your next task: Pop the fig pod, dropping the Electra Ray into the basin. The fish can feed on the flytrap's thorny roots, give the carnivorous plant a good jolt, and thus open the trap. But puncturing a Quaffler Fig is much easier said than done.

Note: The Electra Ray must be sucked through the Quaffler Fig vine system one pod at a time. Therefore, first you must send the fish to the Fig's first spiky pod (just above the vine swing puzzle) before you can send it to the second pod by Saavedro's mural, then on to the third pod over the Venus flytrap's roots.

🦋 Before you leave, look at the edge of the basin just to the left of the branch stairway. See the cables? (They're hard to spot in the murk. See figure 5-28.) Those aren't botanical; they look like electrical wiring, actually.

🦋 Continue along the path as it winds behind and below the fig pod until you reach an imager on the right. Aha!

Prima's Official Strategy Guide

Note: Each of the three Ages has an imager with a separate message from Saavedro. You can visit the Ages (and find the imagers) in any order. But the messages play in the same order regardless of the order you visit the Ages. So Saavedro's first message plays on the first imager you activate, whether on Voltaic, Amateria, or Edanna. The second message plays on the second imager you activate, no matter which Age; and the same goes for the third message on the third imager you activate.

Fig. 5-28. Find the imager tucked behind and below the forest basin.

❤ Approach the imager and push the button. Saavedro has another message for Atrus.

❤ Step back onto the narrow path, turn right, and follow it until it stops at the curled Tongue Fern. Hmmm, no symbiotic spore here, so there's no source of light to unfurl the plant.

❤ Turn around and retrace your route around the fish-filled fig pod and back up the stairs to the mural area.

❤ Turn left at the thorny roots and take the other path. (Just follow the Quaffler Fig vine. See figure 5-29.) It runs above and behind the glowing pod toward some big white flowers hanging on vines.

Fig. 5-29. After you suck the Electra Ray down to the lower pod, climb back up to the mural area and then take the other path to the orchids.

These white flowers are Lambent Orchids. Bright and delicate, the Lambent Orchid reflects light with the intensity of a mirror. Several plants in this dark forest react to light—the Tongue Fern, for one. Your task here is to set up an orchid reflection system to direct sunlight to various targets.

132

primagames.com

Fig. 5-30. The Lambent Orchid's petals are highly reflective. Use them to shoot sunlight at targets.

❦ Stop at the first Lambent Orchid on the right side of the path. Note that its petal "dish" aims directly across the forest, where another orchid and an Aurora Blossom loom above a branch-formed ledge.

❦ Continue down the path to the second Lambent Orchid.

❦ Approach the back of the orchid and click on the small "aperture" near the stem. This gives you a view through the orchid's inner lens.

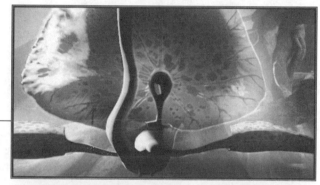

Fig. 5-31. Click the aperture on the backside of a Lambent Orchid to see its "lens view."

Fig. 5-32. Aim the second orchid at the Tongue Fern.

❤ Pivot the orchid until you center the curled Tongue Fern in the lens.

❤ Back away from the lens, turn right, and continue to the third Lambent Orchid (the one in sunlight at the end of the path.)

❤ Look through the orchid's lens. Because the sun hits this flower, you can see the bright spot from its reflective dish.

❤ Pivot the view to the left, putting the hotspot right on the second orchid. (See figure 5-33.)

Now you've got a double-bounce of light. The second orchid throws the sunlight from the first across the forest. If the orchid is positioned correctly, it reflects light at the Tongue Fern, causing that plant to unfurl.

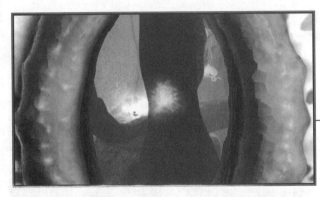

Fig. 5-33. Aim the third orchid's light back at the second orchid (at left). Note for later that this view includes the first orchid (at right), too.

❤ Return to the second orchid and look through its lens to verify that the Tongue Fern has unfurled. If it hasn't, move the hot spot over the fern.

❤ Retrace your route back down the stairs to the basin, then follow the dark path that winds around behind the glowing fig pod, past the imager to to the Tongue Fern. Cross the now-open fern bridge.

❤ On the other side, turn right and climb up through an open, hollowed-out branch. Glowing yellow-orange mushrooms light the way.

Fig. 5-34. Follow the glowing mushrooms to the top of the hollow branch.

❤ At the top, you emerge from the hollow branch onto the ledge where the Aurora Blossom sits.

Notice that somebody hacked away the back petals of the Aurora Blossom, leaving its lens uncovered and locked onto a single view. Approach the big flower to see that it points at the water-laden pod with the Electra Ray below. If you can get sunlight channeled through the Aurora Blossom, you can try the same trick you used up on Deadwood Ridge and pop the pod using lens-focused light.

Fig. 5-35. This damaged Aurora Blossom points down at the swollen fig pod below.

- ❦ Continue past the Aurora Blossom up the stairs to the fourth Lambent Orchid.

- ❦ Look through the orchid's lens and pivot the view until it centers on the Aurora Blossom just below.

- ❦ Return down the stairs and enter the hollow branch.

- ❦ One click down the hollow branch, you reach a fork. (See figure 5-36.)

Fig. 5-36. Here's where the path splits; the upper hollow branch leads to a swing vine, the lower returns to the Tongue Fern bridge.

Here, a second hollow branch arcs above the first and across a tall opening to the outside. This upper path curves to another bungee swing vine that we'll use later. For now, though, let's return to the orchids on the other side of the forest.

- Follow the mushroom-lit lower path leading back down to the Tongue Fern.

- Cross the fern bridge, follow the narrow path all the way back to mural area, then turn left and return to the third Lambent Orchid (the one hanging in the sunlight at the end of the path).

- Pivot this orchid until you center the hot spot on the first orchid (see figure 5-37).

The beam of sunlight now reflects off the first orchid and shoots across the forest to the fourth orchid, which in turn directs the beam into the Aurora Blossom lens. The lens concentrates the sunlight into a burning ray that pierces the pod, spilling its contents into the root-filled basin below.

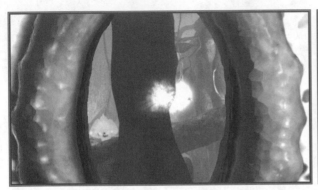

Fig. 5-37. Third to first to fourth! This orchid "triple play" channels light through the Aurora Blossom lens to puncture the pod.

As expected, the hungry Electra Ray immediately feeds on the thorny roots of the Venus flytrap, sending electric jolts up to the big plant. Just like the baby flytrap on Saavedro's work desk in the J'nanin Observatory, the mature plant opens its trap when zapped, releasing the mother Grossamery. Off she goes, back to her nest! And your next task is to follow her lead, somehow.

- After the freed bird flies away, look in the third orchid's aperture again.

- Pivot the hot spot left, back to the second orchid. This unfurls the Tongue Fern again. (You might want to check the view through the second orchid's aperture and verify that the light beam has opened the Tongue Fern.)

- Go back down to the basin, now filled with water and home to the Electra Ray.

- Work your way around behind the basin to the imager and press the button to view Saavedro's message.

- Retrace your route over the Tongue Fern and up the open, hollowed-out branch.

- Proceed up to the spot near the top where you see the ocean to the left through Edanna's outer trunk.

- Turn around and find the frayed opening of the upper hollow branch. Refer back to figure 5-36 to see what it looks like.

- Enter the upper hollow branch. Proceed as it curves sharply to the left and then opens onto a ledge. On the way, you find another one of Saavedro's journal pages.

Note: Make sure to retrieve any journal pages Saavedro has left for you.

- Follow the ledge to the bungee vine.

- Use the swing to drop down to Edanna's lower swamp.

Fig. 5-38. Hop on this bungee vine to drop safely into the Edanna swamp.

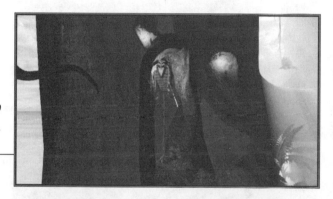

Fig. 5-39. The stairs at right lead up to a Jumping Dragon plant that can lift you back up to the forest.

❤ As you look down the tree branch path in front of you, notice the smooth path on the left side and the stairway carved into the branch on the right.

❤ Climb the steps and proceed to a big, flat-leafed plant.

This is a coiled Jumping Dragon. It springs upward if you stand on it, lifting you to the branch with the bungee vine swing. In this walkthrough, you don't have to use this plant. But it's nice to know you have a way back up.

OK, OK, go ahead, give it a couple of tries, just for fun.

Fig. 5-40. Want some spring in your step? Hop aboard this Jumping Dragon for a ride back up to the bungee vine.

❤ Return to the spot where you dropped down on the bungee vine.

❤ This time, take the smooth path to the left.

❤ Follow the path through the root-formed arch into the swamp.

Fig. 5-41. This natural archway leads into the Edanna swamp.

Edanna Swamp

The murky, low-lit swamp sits at the very base of Edanna. Here, the giant tree's root system snakes in and out of saltwater, forming uneven paths. Shafts of sunlight occasionally break through the forest canopy or gaps in the great outer trunk, but luminescent growths provide much of the lighting in this area.

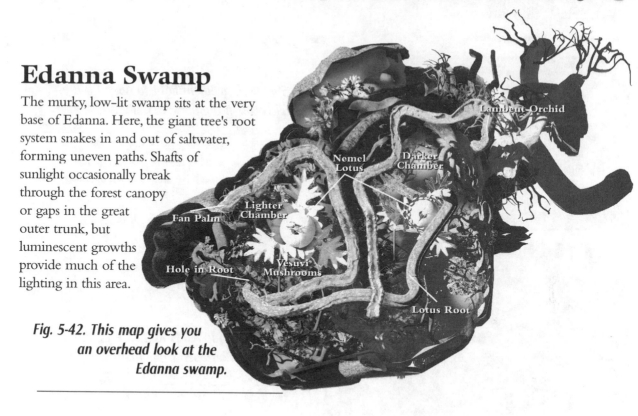

Fig. 5-42. This map gives you an overhead look at the Edanna swamp.

A huge, twisted clump of roots divides the swamp into two chambers. The first chamber you enter receives almost no direct sunlight, so we'll call it the "darker chamber." The second is more open and airy, so let's call it the "lighter chamber."

Darker Chamber

A large Nemel Lotus lies dormant in the center of the darker chamber. This plant contains the succulents the mother Grossamery needs to feed her hatchling; however, they're locked inside the plant's tightly closed pod. To expose the Nemel Lotus's fruit pod, you need two stimuli: first, *sunlight* to induce the stamen filaments to unfurl atop the pod (thus exposing the anther, the pollen-producing part of the plant), and second, *pollinating insects* which swarm to the scent, inciting the pod's petals to open.

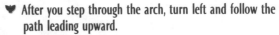
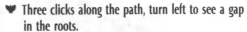

Fig. 5-43. You need sunlight to open up the Nemel Lotus in the darker chamber.

- After you step through the arch, turn left and follow the path leading upward.
- Three clicks along the path, turn left to see a gap in the roots.

Fig. 5-44. This gap leads to a second, lighter chamber with an open Nemel Lotus.

Through the gap you can see part of another Nemel Lotus, this one fully opened. It sits in the second chamber (the lighter chamber). We'll visit it in a moment. For now continue up the darker chamber path.

- Continue up the rising path as it curves around the Nemel Lotus.
- The path eventually leads up to a Lambent Orchid hanging down the outside of Edanna's trunk. It sits in sunlight, so you can use its reflective quality.
- Step behind the orchid and look through its aperture.
- Pivot the hot spot until it hits the flowers atop the Nemel Lotus below.

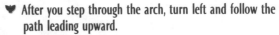
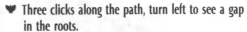

Fig. 5-45. Follow the path to this Lambent Orchid, then aim its light right at the stamen filaments atop the Nemel Lotus.

Note how the stamen filaments atop the Nemel Lotus immediately unfurl in the reflected sunlight. These can attract the flying insects needed to stimulate the plant's large pod to open, thus revealing the succulent fruit. But do you see any insects yet? No, because they're all buzzing around the Nemel Lotus that's already open in the other chamber (the one you saw through the root gap).

Your next task: Lure the insects into this chamber.

- ❤ Return down the path to the gap in the roots. (Remember, on the way down it's now on your right side.)

- ❤ Walk through the gap into the other chamber.

Lighter Chamber

You emerge into the second root-formed chamber. See? It's not as gloomy in here. In one very prominent sunbeam, another Nemel Lotus sits wide open, its succulents either crushed or missing, taken by the mother Grossamery before she was trapped by the Venus flytrap plant. A swarm of pollinating insects flies around the lotus's unfurled stamen filaments. The insects will not leave this chamber so long as the filaments are extended.

Fig. 5-46. This second Nemel Lotus is open, thanks to that shaft of sunlight from the right and a swarm of pollinating insects on top.

❤ Turn right and follow the path around the Nemel Lotus up to the retracted Fan Palm.

❤ Touch the heart of the Fan Palm to raise and spread its big fronds.

Fig. 5-47. Open this Fan Palm to block the sunlight shining on the Nemel Lotus below.

The Fan Palm's fronds now block the light shining through the gap in the trunk. Deprived of sunlight, the stamen filaments atop the Nemel Lotus curl up. At the same time, the pod petals close tightly. But the goofy insects won't leave. How can we get them to vacate the area and go pollinate the Nemel Lotus over in the first chamber?

- Turn around and follow the path that curves around the Nemel Lotus to the other side of the chamber.

- Approach a thick, purplish root with a hole cleanly bored in it. Near the hole sits a ball-shaped Vesuvi Mushroom.

- Touch the Vesuvi Mushroom. A cloud of noxious spores shoots upward.

Fig. 5-48. See the Vesuvi Mushrooms next to the Nemel Lotus? They emit spores that insects really, really hate.

- Turn around and walk toward the Nemel Lotus.

- When you reach the pod, look down to find more Vesuvi Mushrooms.

- Touch the biggest Vesuvi Mushroom to fire up a cloud. Repelled by the spores, the insects immediately swarm out of the chamber.

Note: The insect swarm exits this chamber only if the stamen filaments atop the Nemel Lotus are closed for lack of sunlight. Therefore, if you touch the Vesuvi Mushroom while the sun is shining on the Nemel Lotus—that is, with the Fan Palm closed—the insects fly up, wait for the spores to settle, and then fly back down to continue pollinating the plant.

Fig. 5-49. Enter the hole in this hollow purple root. It leads right into the pod of the first Nemel Lotus.

- Now enter the hole in the big purple root. It's hollow and big enough for you to walk through.

- Follow the root tunnel. Along the way, look for another page of Saavedro's journal.

- You emerge directly inside the first Nemel Lotus! The walls of the plant are lined with fruit.

- Look up and turn until you see the two stamen filaments, now abuzz with insects.

- Click to move toward the filaments, then turn around to see the huge succulent fruit.

Fig. 5-50. Ever been in a pod before? If so, you already know about grabbing this stem.

The juicy Nemel Lotus succulents and their vines form a curving "cage" that the mother Grossamery can pick up and carry to her nest. See those handle-like stems attached to the fruit cage? As the fruit ripens, it distends enough to push the stem, which then shoots seeds with a loud popping noise; this sound informs the bird that the succulents are available.

You could hang around in the pod until the fruit is fully ripe.

Or you could be proactive.

- Climb up into the succulent cage.

- Pull one of the stems. (They look like big handles.)

Seeds fly skyward and a loud *pop* reverberates in the pod. The mother Grossamery, hearing this signal, swoops in and grabs the fruit cage in her claws. She carries it, along with you, on an exhilarating joyride up to her nest.

Fig. 5-51. Here's a bird's eye view of your joyride up to the nest atop Edanna.

The Grossamery Nest

The nest sits atop one of the oldest inward-curving branches in Edanna. Over time, predatory Strangler Figs surrounded this branch, encasing it in a network of vines that grew inward, strangling the older wood and eating it away. Many vines have aged and broken away, but a large tangle still hangs beneath the bird's nest. Sap from the dying branch filled this cluster, hardened to opacity, and, in combination with the Strangler vines, formed Edanna's special Nature symbol.

Fig. 5-52. After the birds feed, you're free to head down to the vine chamber below.

Fig. 5-53. Here's the Nature symbol.

- Pivot left and exit the cage by sliding down the curving bough beneath.

- Look at the Nature symbol formed by vine fragments encased in amber.

- Click on the symbol. You automatically sketch it on a sheet of paper.

- Turn and use the J'nanin linking book to return to the second floor of the Observatory.

Back to J'nanin

When you return to J'nanin from Edanna with the Energy symbol, you link directly into the second floor of the Observatory. If you've followed the order of this walkthrough, you've found the last Age symbol and are ready to visit Narayan.

❤ Approach the imaging table.

❤ Take your sketch of the Nature symbol from inventory and put it on the imaging table.

Fig. 3-54. Take the Nature symbol sketch from inventory and place it on the imaging table.

The imager projects the sketch downward, raising a three-dimensional representation of the symbol from a cam beneath the table. Another cam drops down, imprinting the 3-D symbol on its elastic surface. Then the cams rotate, manipulating the cage mechanism.

If you're following this walkthrough, Edanna is the last Element Age you visit. Thus, placing the journal page on the imaging table extends the ramp across the pit to the open cage. When it locks into place, a hologram projector message from Atrus to his sons plays on the ceiling. (See the Note on the following page.)

Fig. 3-55. Perhaps Sirris and Achenar didn't take this message in the spirit it was intended....

Note: Remember you can bring back symbols from the Ages *in any order*. When placed on the imaging table, each symbol activates some aspect of the cage mechanism in the pit, then triggers a hologram message. Whether from Voltaic, Amateria, or Edanna, the first symbol placed on the imaging table raises the cage from the pit, the second symbol opens the cage, and the third symbol extends a ramp to the cage. The hologram messages play in the same order regardless of the order you solve the Ages.

Fig. 3-56. Cross the ramp and use the Narayan book.

🦅 Cross the ramp to the Narayan linking book.

🦅 Open the book and touch the panel to link to the game's final Age.

Chapter 6
Narayan
The Age of Balance

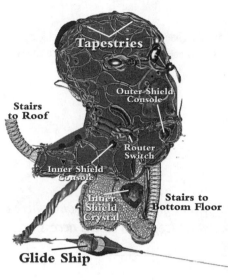

Fig. 6-1. Here's where you arrive: the middle floor of the Narayan linking chamber.

Narayan is a water world; to survive here, a civilization must manage symbiotic elements of the Age's unique ecosystem. (For more on Narayan, see Chapter 8, Historian's Journal.) Your link from J'nanin drops you into an organic-looking, split-level chamber. Dark veins run through translucent walls. Thick roots twist into pillars and stairs, then fan out across the floor and ceiling to form sturdy, crisscrossing support beams. Behind you, five pairs of red tapestries hang on the wall. Each tapestry is embroidered with words and symbols. Note that another set of tapestries appears to have been torn from the wall.

- 𝔗 Note the gold symbols on the tapestries decorating the walls. They look strangely familiar.
- 𝔗 Climb the four green stairs to the raised part of the room.
- 𝔗 Examine the devices here. A router switch sits between a pair of low podiums.
- 𝔗 Try to activate either podium by clicking on it. Aside from a weak hum, nothing significant happens. Apparently, these devices lack power.

Fig. 6-2. These podiums and their router switch need electricity. Better find a power source.

☂ Turn around and approach the window barred by a vine trellis. See the glide ship—the gondola-like vehicle hanging from a cable? The doorway to the glide ship platform is just to your left, but a translucent ice shield blocks the way.

☂ Turn right and exit the chamber.

☂ Climb the metal stairway to the roof.

Fig. 6-3. Surely that glide ship goes somewhere interesting. But an ice shield blocks access.

Chamber Roof

Fig. 6-4. Here's an overhead view of the roof of the Narayan linking chamber. Note: The glide ship platform and inner shield, though seen here, are on the middle floor level.

Wow. The small ice shield you saw downstairs has a massive counterpart, one that extends around the entire Narayan linking chamber. From this vantage point you also see the grand scale of the billowing organic structure: green, gas–filled spore sacs entwined by a latticework of thick roots. Indeed, the root spacing is so even it looks deliberately woven. Could this be one of the Lattice Trees mentioned in Saavedro's journal and hologram messages?

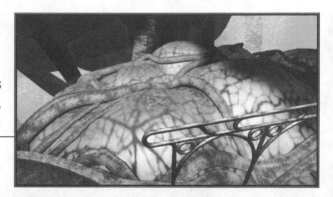

Fig. 6-5. The lattice roots form netlike enclosures for the floating spore sacs.

Across the roof, a tall metal tower topped by a blue glowing crystal rises. (See the sidebar on "How the Narayan Shields Work" for an explanation of this crystal's function.) Below to your right, the glide ship hangs from a cable that runs through the ice shield. Two rows of electrical circuit coils (marking the chamber's power core, no doubt) are stacked to the left. In front of you, under a round grated platform, orange mist glows—energy channeled up the core from geothermal vents on the ocean floor.

Fig. 6-6. These circuit coils mean electricity is nearby. In fact, a generator powered by geothermal vents is below you.

How the Narayan Shields Work

By Phil Saunders, Creative Director for *Myst III: Exile*

Like the water on Riven, water in Narayan has special properties Atrus has learned to control—in this case, the eternal mists and sea of clouds that blanket the Age. Atrus installed special blue crystals in the linking chamber. Each crystal in its natural state generates a harmonic that excites the water molecules in the surrounding mists, causing them to bond and form an impenetrable shield of ice in a perfect sphere around the crystal.

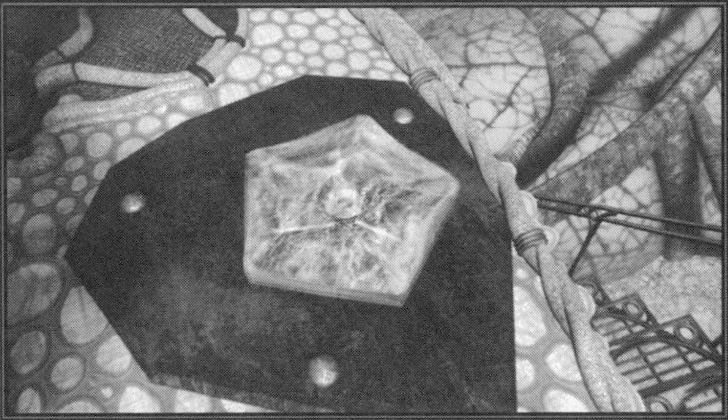

Fig. 6-7. These special Amateria crystals generate the inner and outer ice shields.

These crystals were mined on Amateria, as you might expect. (In fact, Amateria is the source of many crystals with special properties.) The big one that generates the outer shield glows atop the tower. (You see it if you look up from the roof.) The small one that generates the inner shield is embedded in the floor of the gondola platform, just outside the doorway.

To lower the shield, Atrus taps into the geothermal vents below the tree to power a generator (the large cylindrical device you stand on in Narayan). This, in turn, sends a current to one of two crystals, directed by the routing switch in the upper tapestry chamber. The current serves to stabilize the crystal, allowing the shield to dissipate.

The art is similar to that which Atrus applied in Amateria, but substantially more flexible due to the special properties of water in Narayan. Ice spheres in Amateria are quite fragile and susceptible to harmonic vibrations. Because of this, they're limited in diameter, and also will not form naturally into a sphere, but must be molded by a rotating Water Lathe.

- **Step onto the round, grated platform.**
- **This triggers an automatic confrontation with Saavedro, who enters through the metal door.**

Fig. 6-8. Saavedro's not happy, and that's not good, because he carries a big hammer.

> **Note:** Doesn't Saavedro's cloak look familiar? Did you notice the missing tapestry torn from the wall downstairs?

Saavedro is a bit distressed that you're not Atrus. He browbeats himself awhile, in particular asking, "Why would he rewrite Narayan?" Poor Saavedro believes that Atrus has the godlike ability to resurrect an Age gone sour. Finally, he turns to you again. He points out that you're stuck here with him; he left his J'nanin linking book in Tomahna. And with distinct menace, he strongly suggests that if you find a way to link out of Narayan, you'd best keep an eye over your shoulder.

- ☥ After Saavedro leaves, look down to your right and spot the handle on the floor.
- ☥ Pull the handle to activate the power core. Electricity now flows into the chamber below.
- ☥ Take the stairs back down to the middle floor.

Fig. 6-9. Twist the floor handle to this position to power up the devices downstairs.

Middle Floor: The Inner Shield Code

Electricity flows now though the router switch. But the router sends power to only one podium at a time (the one to which the router's handle points). Right now, the router switch points right, sending power to the rightmost podium. But if you try to manipulate the console display on that podium, nothing happens.

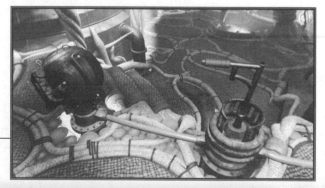

Fig. 6-10. First, route power to the leftmost control podium.

☥ Click on the router switch to flip it left, routing power to the left podium.

☥ Walk around to the front of the leftmost podium and click on it to raise it. A small metal hatch covers the top.

☥ Click on the hatch to uncover the console.

☥ Click on various parts of the console display.

Note three clusters that represent three symbols. Each symbol comprises four glyphs. Each of those four glyphs looks similar to the ones on the tapestries. Indeed, the symbols you found on Voltaic, Amateria, and Edanna each appear to comprise these tapestry glyphs too. When Atrus devised the three symbols to conceal in his Lesson Age course, he composed each symbol from four smaller Narayan glyphs.

However, when devising a plan to lure Atrus back to Narayan, Saavedro decided to alter Atrus' three Age symbols, "erasing" part of each one in some way. Thus, when you found them, you obtained only *partial* symbols—a fact that becomes important here in Narayan. Each Age symbol lacks some glyphs, so you must figure out what's missing.

How can you determine the missing glyphs? Start with the Age symbols you have.

☥ Study the tapestries on the wall. Notice that each Age symbol comprises two of the glyphs before you.

☥ Find the words that correspond to the glyphs in the Age symbols.

You find that the Voltaic glyphs stand for the words "Future" and "Motion," the Amateria glyphs stand for "Force" and "Change," and the Edanna glyphs mean "Nature" and "Encourage." Why do those words sound so familiar? Of course! They're parts of the Age-building tenets you've been carrying with you in Atrus' journal since the very beginning of your adventure:

☥ Energy powers future motion.

☥ Nature encourages mutual dependence.

☥ Dynamic forces spur change.

☥ Balanced systems stimulate civilization.

Now you can complete the four-part symbols you need to enter in the control console. Simply find the glyphs for the missing words from the first three phrases.

♈ Reread these journal phrases again, and identify the two missing words in the symbols for Voltaic, Amateria, and Edanna. By comparing the two words you know from each Age's symbol to the corresponding mantra, you can complete the sentences.

♈ Scan the chamber tapestries again to locate the glyphs that match these missing key words.

Fig. 6-11. The Voltaic Age symbol is made from the Narayan glyphs for the words "Future" and "Motion." So the missing words from Atrus' Energy mantra are "Energy" and "Power."

Fig. 6-12. The Amateria Age symbol is made from the Narayan glyphs for the words "Force" and "Change." So the missing words from Atrus' Dynamic Forces mantra are "Dynamic" and "Spur."

Fig. 6-13. The Edanna Age symbol is made from the Narayan glyphs for the words "Nature" and "Encourage." So the missing words from Atrus' Nature mantra are "Mutual" and "Dependence."

But how do the glyphs fit together?

First of all, note that you input only one Age symbol at a time. You build the symbol by recreating each of its four Narayan glyphs in one of the three "clusters" of the podium. To recreate the four glyphs of each symbol, click on segments of the cluster.

But which glyph goes in which corner of each cluster?

☨ Examine the Age sketches in your inventory. From their arrangement, you can see that the top glyph in a symbol stands for the first word in the phrase, and the phrase continues clockwise in a circle.

☨ Input the Narayan tapestry glyphs for the Energy mantra starting with Energy at the top, then continuing clockwise with Power, Future, and Motion.

Note: You can input the three symbols in any order.

☨ Input the Narayan tapestry glyphs for the Nature mantra starting with Nature at the top, then continuing clockwise with Encourage, Mutual, and Dependence.

☨ Input the Narayan tapestry glyphs for the Dynamic Forces mantra starting with Dynamic at the top, then continuing clockwise with Force, Spur, and Change. When the last symbol is entered, the console locks, and the inner shield comes down. Cool!

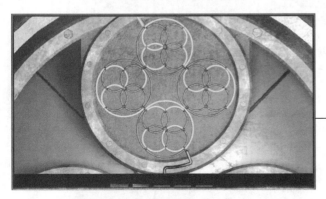

Fig. 6-14. Here's the final Energy symbol entered in the podium console.

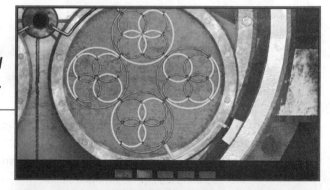

Fig. 6-15. Here's the final Nature symbol entered in the podium console.

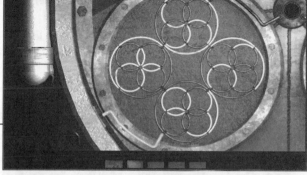

Fig. 6-16. Here's the final Dynamic Forces symbol entered in the podium console.

Fig. 6-17. The inner shield melts!

Note: Once you lock the correct code into the left console, the inner shield melts whenever you route power to that console. So you can raise or lower the shield by turning the router switch.

☂ Go to the router switch and route power to the other (rightmost) podium. The inner shield reforms itself.

☂ Approach the other podium. This one, obviously, controls the outer shield.

☂ Raise the podium and open the hatch to see the console.

Hmmm, only one symbol to enter here. No doubt it works like the other podium code. Of course, you've already used Atrus' mantras for Energy, Dynamic Forces, and Nature to determine which glyphs to enter on the inner shield podium. So the remaining Age-building tenet—*balanced systems stimulate civilization*—must indicate the symbol code for this outer shield console. Saavedro could never figure out the second shield puzzle because he never had access to Atrus' mantras—only you, Sirrus, and Achenar knew Atrus' last mantra.

If you look at the tapestries, you'll find the symbols for the words "balance" and "system." But where are the rest of the corresponding glyphs for the mantra words? Downstairs.

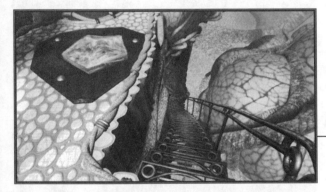

Fig. 6-18. With the inner shield down, you can access these stairs from the glide ship platform down to the bottom floor.

☂ Locate the glyphs for "balance" and "system" on the first floor tapestries before heading downstairs.

☂ Turn the router switch left to melt the inner shield again.

☂ Step through the unblocked passage to the glide ship balcony and look around. Obviously, this craft goes nowhere until that outer shield comes down, too.

☂ Note the blue crystal imbedded in the floor. This generates the inner shield. (See the sidebar "How the Narayan Shields Work" for more on this.)

☂ Turn left and go down the stairs to the bottom floor.

Bottom Floor: The Outer Shield Code

The lower tapestry room is similar to the one upstairs. Five more pairs of red tapestries with symbols and words hang on the back wall. But just inside the entry is an item of particular interest: a linking book to Tomahna! This must be the one Saavedro uses on his expeditions to spy on Atrus.

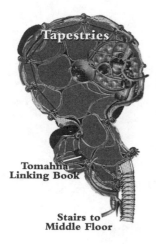

Fig. 6-19. Here's the simple layout of the bottom floor of the Narayan linking chamber.

♉ Approach the Tomahna linking book.

♉ Take the book. It goes into inventory. But don't use it yet!

Fig. 6-20. Take the Tomahna linking book, but don't use it yet.

Why not just high-tail it out of here right now? Two reasons: First, you haven't yet acquired what you've sought the entire game—the Releeshahn book. Second, remember Saavedro's not-so-veiled warning: "If you *do* find a way out of here, I suggest that you think very carefully about using it. Because the one thing I know about linking books—the doors they open don't close behind you." In other words, if you leave, he will follow. With his hammer. And a very, very bad attitude.

Note: Once you gain the Tomahna linking book, you can use it at any time. But if you return to Atrus while Saavedro is still free to roam the Narayan linking chamber, Saavedro follows you to Tomahna—and the consequences are quite unpleasant for you and your friends there.

☥ Find the glyphs for "stimulate" and "civilization" on the downstairs tapestries.

☥ Translate the Balance mantra into glyphs—"balanced systems stimulate civilization."

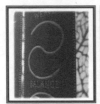 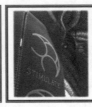 

Fig. 6-21. The Narayan Age symbol is made from four Narayani glyphs, the two found upstairs–"Balance" and "System"—and two found downstairs— "Stimulate" and "Civilization."

☥ Return upstairs to the router switch.

☥ Turn the router switch to the right, routing power to the outer shield console. The inner shield reforms over the doorway to the glide ship.

☥ Input the Narayan tapestry glyphs for the Balance mantra starting with Balance at the top, then continuing clockwise with System, Stimulate, and Civilization. When the symbol is entered, the console locks, and the outer shield comes down.

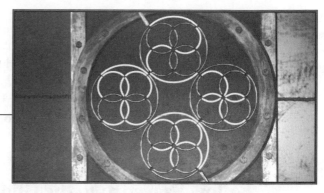

Fig. 6-22. Here's the final Balance symbol entered in the podium console.

Voilà! The outer shield melts away! The podium code locks in, too. Now, whenever the router switch points right, the outer shield melts and the inner shield goes up. When the switch points left, the inner shield melts, but the outer shield goes up. Thus, only one shield at a time can be eliminated—which soon creates an interesting dilemma.

Endgame Scenarios

When you enter the fourth symbol into the console, the outer shield melts. Saavedro runs in, overjoyed to see that Narayan is still alive—indeed, the cheery lights of a settlement glow on a distant Lattice Tree. But when Saavedro experiments with the router switch, he grasps its double-lock system—and realizes he needs you to lower the outer shield while he is in the glide ship. In return, he'll give you Releeshahn—or so he says. Then he goes out to the glide ship platform.

Here's where the *Myst III: Exile* endgame branches into numerous possibilities.

Immediately Throw the Router Switch

Fig. 6-23. If you do as Saavedro says and open the outer shield immediately, he double-crosses you!

If you simply take Saavedro at his word and throw the router switch to drop the outer shield, he double-crosses you. Makes sense, doesn't it? The poor fellow has been in exile, building a deep store of hatred and mistrust, for nearly a quarter of a century. When the shield melts, Saavedro makes a snide remark about "my end of the bargain." Then he simply tosses the Releeshahn book into the sea, hops aboard the glide ship, and rides happily to the Narayan settlement—leaving you to link back to Tomahna and face the intense disappointment of Atrus and Catherine.

Follow Saavedro to the Glide Ship

Fig. 6-24. Saavedro's in no mood for small talk. He can tolerate some delay, but eventually he'll snap if you hang out on the glide ship platform too long.

If you distrust Saavedro (rightly so) and follow him out to the glide ship, he grows angry and threatens to drop the Releeshahn book into the sea below. After that, several possibilities present themselves, all pretty bad.

1. If you linger on the glide ship platform, Saavedro holds the book over the ocean below and gives you one last warning. If you still take no action, Saavedro finally drops the book and attacks you with his hammer. Game over!

2. If you leave the platform after his first warning, but then return to the glide ship a second time, Saavedro holds the book over the ocean and gives you a last warning. If you still take no action, Saavedro finally drops the book and attacks you. Game over!

3. If you leave the platform *twice* after Saavedro's warnings, then foolishly return a *third* time—well, you really tick him off, and understandably so. On your third trip out, Saavedro turns and springs without warning right at your sorry face.

Shut Down the Power

Fig. 6-25. Here's a good move! Flip the power switch to trap Saavedro between the shields. Now he's at your mercy.

This should be your first action after Saavedro goes out to the glide ship. If you head upstairs to the roof and pull the handle to shut off power to the shield consoles, both shields automatically activate, trapping Saavedro between them. This is a good first move. But bad moves are still possible after you shut off power. For example, if you foolishly flip the power back on, the inner shield melts again, and Saavedro runs angrily upstairs to hammer-whack you. Here are some other possibilities.

Go Back Downstairs

Fig. 6-26. Saavedro, knowing he's trapped, offers you what you want.

If you shut off power and go back downstairs to look at Saavedro through the vine trellis window, he approaches and begs for your mercy, then hands you the Releeshahn book. Now you've got him where you want him. But mistakes are still possible.

1. If you forget to flip the router switch to the right (toward the outer shield console) before you go back upstairs, the inner shield melts when you turn on the power. Saavedro feels betrayed and pounds upstairs to hammer you.

2. If you immediately link back to Tomahna with the Releeshahn book, you leave Saavedro trapped between the ice shields.

The latter choice is certainly a legitimate one. Your experience reveals Saavedro to be an unstable man full of violent anger and fully bent on vengeance—a man too dangerous perhaps to set free. But consider the larger moral implications of any decision here. If you do strand Saavedro and return to Tomahna, Atrus is happy to regain access to his D'ni brethren, but the

game ends with a bittersweet voiceover in which he laments "the anguish of decisions that were made." Ultimately, Atrus asks, "But if I had been the one to face Saavedro…would I have left him stranded without hope? Would I have sacrificed his dreams to claim my own?"

Set Saavedro Free

Fig. 6-27. After he gives you the Releeshahn book, why not set the poor soul free?

Of course, the best ending is the most humane one—the one Atrus surely would have chosen himself. After Saavedro goes out to the glide ship:

- ☥ Run upstairs and shut off the power.

- ☥ Go back downstairs and retrieve the Releeshahn book from the sad, trapped man.

- ☥ Flip the router switch to the outer shield (rightmost) console.

- ☥ Go back upstairs and turn on the power.

Saavedro rides joyously to the Lattice Tree settlement in the distance. Finally, link back to Tomahna to deliver the book to Atrus. You hear his final voiceover comments in which he rejoices that "old wrongs have finally been righted."

Fig. 6-28. Atrus and Catherine appreciate your efforts on their behalf...and Atrus adds another chapter to his journal, content that "old wrongs have finally been righted."

Chapter 7
Soft Hints

When you buy a strategy guide, you seek answers. But some guide buyers want more than answers—well, to be precise, *less* than answers, actually. Yes, many fans of the *Myst* universe crave the satisfaction of solving puzzles themselves. They don't want a road map. When lost, they want a quick head bob indicating "you might want to try over there."

Fig. 7-1. How the heck does this thing work? In this chapter, we give you hints, not answers.

So we've designed a chapter for you folks who don't desire the firm hand–holding of our Golden Path walkthroughs and instead prefer a gentle nudge or two in the right direction. After all, even the most experienced puzzle fiend can get stuck in the clever conundrums of the Ages of Atrus, the great puzzle master himself.

Important! Read the next section carefully to see how it works, lest you end up acquiring more knowledge than you sought.

How to Use Puzzle Hints

This chapter is designed to give you layers of hints for each puzzle. By "layers" we mean this: We provide a series of hints, moving from general to specific, without giving away the final solution. Here's how it works:

- ◀ Under each Age, we list the main locations/puzzles. Remember, though, that *Myst III: Exile* is a very non-linear game. You can visit the Ages in any order, and encounter puzzles in a myriad of different ways.

- ◀ Under each location within an Age, we list a series of questions that explorers might logically ask.

- ◀ Then, under each question, we give a bullet-point list of increasingly more specific answers, but always stop short of revealing the final solution.

Again, each bullet point under a particular question reveals more than the previous bullet point. So, for those of you with wild eyes or no willpower, we suggest covering each stack of bullet points with a sheet of titanium-reinforced paper stock to eliminate the possibility of what we in the industry call "seeing ahead."

If you reach the end of a bulleted list and *still* can't solve the puzzle, don't be ashamed. Simply refer to the corresponding chapter and section in "The Golden Path Walkthrough." Hey, it's OK. People cheat all the time. We got all of our puzzle solutions directly from the developer, Presto Studios, and yet we still feel really good about ourselves.

General Hints

Before you jump into the Ages, take a look at this quick list of starter tips.

- Like its predecessors *Myst* and *Riven*, *Myst III: Exile* is a game of exploration. Pay close attention to the details of each Age; don't overlook anything!

- Don't assume that toys or gadgets are mere eye candy. Many simplistic devices you find early in the game provide clues for later, more complex puzzles.

Fig. 7-2. Gadgets like these on Saavedro's desk provide hints for later puzzles.

- Read everything! If someone hands you or leaves a journal during the course of the game, take time to read every page. Journals do more than provide rich back-story; they provide important clues, too.

- Saavedro scattered a number of his journal pages around the Ages, too. Watch for them; they explain a lot about his motivation.

- Each Age has a predominant theme. When stuck, think about that theme. For example, in an Age that exhibits mechanical notions, think mechanically—look for gadgets, see how they interact, and so forth. If nature is the overall theme, think "natural"—look for life forms that can solve your problems.

- Puzzle goals are readily apparent in *Exile*, and the rewards for achieving them are immediate and gratifying. This doesn't mean the puzzles are *easy*, by any means. But for the most part, the puzzle-solving in *Exile* is straightforward and intuitive. Don't out-think yourself!

Hints for J'nanin: The Lesson Age

J'nanin is a hub world; it links to all the other Ages in *Myst III: Exile*. Solve J'nanin's puzzles to gain access to those Ages. Each J'nanin puzzle relates to the theme of the Age you seek to access. In general, then, look for interactive puzzle elements that seem related by theme.

The Observatory

Saavedro locked the door off the high bridge at the top of the Observatory, the tall structure in the middle of the island's caldera. If you peek through the window in that door, you see the man pacing around—waiting, apparently. Now what?

How can I get inside the Observatory?

🗡 Look for another entrance.

🗡 Take a trip around the island perimeter. Surely there's another way in.

🗡 Work your way down into the caldera to the freshwater lake below.

🗡 Try that stained-glass greenhouse.

The Observatory elevator is turned the wrong way when I take it to the second floor. How does it rotate?

🗡 Try sending the elevator upstairs without you. Watch its mechanisms.

🗡 Send the elevator up, then check out the empty shaft. See anything interesting?

🗡 Note the evidence of tampering in the shaft. Resetting the mechanisms there requires a guide—preferably, an illustrated one.

🗡 Did you find Saavedro's journal in his room? Try reading it.

🗡 Look for references to mechanisms in Saavedro's journal.

🗡 Look for sketches in Saavedro's journal.

🗡 Do you see anything that looks familiar in Saavedro's journal? If so, note its exact configuration.

Fig. 7-3. Scan Saavedro's journal to find clues to the Observatory elevator puzzle.

I got to the Observatory's second level, but Saavedro linked away. How can I follow him?

- You've got a *lot* of work to do yet.

- Look for messages from Saavedro to get you started.

- Look for buttons that might activate devices.

- The cage in the pit below holds the linking book Saavedro used. Before you can access it, you must solve most of the puzzles in *Myst III: Exile*!

These Observatory telescopes are fun, but what am I looking for?

- First of all, examine the viewing lens itself.

- Focus on what seems most prominent in each telescope's viewing range.

- Find the tusk tower in each view.

- Note the surroundings, so you know which tusk is which. There's a connection between each tusk and the particular telescope that views it.

- Do you see anything interesting on the tusk?

- Do you see anything on the tusk that suggests a way to align your view?

- Note what happens to the telescope itself when you manipulate the zoom, focus, or pan controls.

Are those little marbles that move around the telescope viewing lens important?

⊰ Yes.

⊰ Very important.

⊰ Keep an eye out for similar mechanisms elsewhere on the island.

The Energy Puzzle

How do I enter the tusk that has five buttons on the door?

⊰ Push the buttons in the correct order.

⊰ This is the Energy Age tusk. Solve J'nanin's Energy puzzle to find the door button code.

⊰ Examine the object in front of the door. It looks like a scope with the lens aimed at the buttons.

⊰ Hint: It's a prism. But no light shines through it yet.

⊰ Find a source of light somewhere on (or slightly off) the island.

⊰ Direct the light to the prism.

What's the purpose of those odd poles with view-scopes and differently colored fire marbles on top?

⊰ Each pole has three scopes set at 120-degree angles. Look in each scope to see how the views reflect to and from other scopes on the pole. Which views connect, and which don't?

⊰ Use the reflecting angles of the scopes to direct light from pole to pole.

⊰ We did say direct the light to the prism, didn't we?

Fig. 7-4. Two scopes atop the poles reflect views through each other at 120 angles. The third scope's view is blocked.

I managed to direct the light beam from the offshore gun to the prism. The door looks nice, but now what?

- What does the light do to the door buttons?

- Push the buttons in the order of the color code.

- Can you think of a "color order" you recently followed?

- Follow the light beam.

I got inside the tusk, but how do I reach the linking book?

- Have you seen this linking book chamber through one of the Observatory telescopes yet? If not, head up to the Observatory's second floor for a peek.

- What happens to the Observatory telescope as you pan, focus, and zoom the view on the tusk's linking book chamber?

- In the tusk, look at the podium below the linking book. Does that mechanism look familiar?

- Where else have you seen metal marbles moving around concentric circle tracks?

The Dynamic Forces Puzzle

A big metal weight blocks access to the tusk rising above the rock outcropping just off the main island. How do I move it?

◄ It's round. Surely it rolls.

◄ But the metal weight is too heavy for you to roll. You need a mechanism.

◄ The weight sits on a jointed bridge.

◄ The bridge is moveable. Move it!

◄ Use the bridge controls to move the bridge and roll the weight out of way.

◄ *What* bridge controls, you ask? Didn't you search high and low around the rock outcropping?

◄ Find the ladder that leads to the bridge control podium and go to work.

I got the tusk door open. How can I cross the ripped-out floor to the podium under the linking book?

◄ Fill the hole.

◄ Look at the floor hole. Is anything around here big enough to fill that space?

◄ Is that big, hole-filling thing moveable? Have you moved it before?

How do I reach the Amateria linking book?

◄ Same way you reached the Voltaic linking book. (See "The Energy Puzzle" above.)

The Nature Puzzle

How do I enter the tusk just across from the Observatory? Its door is 30 feet up!

◄ Grow a bridge to it.

◄ Explore the lakefront area down at the caldera's bottom. See any interesting life forms?

◄ Don't be afraid to touch. Nothing will bite.

◄ The little white Squee needs a bridge to his favorite food. Give him a hand.

◄ Watch what happens when the Squee gets to the reddish buds of the Barnacle Moss.

❧ Hmmm. The Moss buds seemed to expand at the sound of the Squee's chirp. Have you seen those buds anywhere else?

Fig. 7-5. Notice the thick growth of Barnacle Moss on the cliff near the seemingly unreachable Nature tusk door.

The Barnacle Moss buds along the cliff wall near the tusk door would make a nice bridge. How can I make them expand?

❧ You can't, but the Squee can.

❧ You need the Squee's chirp to expand the Barnacle Moss.

How do I get the Squee up the ladder to the Barnacle Moss?

❧ You don't need the Squee. You need its chirp.

❧ Climb up the ladder from the caldera's bottom to the first ledge and explore.

❧ Find a hearing aid.

❧ Step up behind the big Hearken Fern and point it at things.

❧ Listen! Everything's amplified.

❧ Find a familiar little sound.

How do I reach the Edanna linking book?

❧ Same way you reached the Voltaic linking book. (See "The Energy Puzzle" above.)

Hints for Voltaic: Age of Energy

This Age embodies power flow that channels raw energy into useful forms. Your overall goal is to complete a circuit linking everything on the island. In general, then, look for breaks in the circuit and determine how to reconnect them. The raw energy sources on Voltaic are water and lava. Your challenge is to convert these into hydroelectricity, electromagnetism, and superheated, pressurized air.

Arrival

I can't open the big door on the stone structure. Is it locked?

- Not exactly. The door opens mechanically.

- The door needs power.

- Make electricity flow to the door.

- In fact, nothing in this Age operates without power. Find the power plant.

Power Plant

Where is the power plant?

- You can see it from your point of arrival.

- It extends from the main island and dams the inlet.

- Follow the catwalk.

- Look for tunnels.

I found it. Now where do I start?

- Hydroelectric power plants convert kinetic energy (energy created by mechanical motion) into electricity by use of turbines. According to *Webster's*, turbines are "rotary engines actuated by the impulse of a current of fluid (say, water) over a series of curved vanes on a central rotating spindle."

- Start by identifying the two basic mechanisms of the power plant: the *waterwheel* (where the energy is created) and the *gear platform* (where the energy is converted).

- Link the two mechanisms.

- Once linked, the mechanisms need motion!

Fig. 7-6. To get power generating, mesh the two big gears here at the gear platform.

Where's the waterwheel? How can I make it turn?

- It's cylindrical and very big. Really, it's hard to miss.

- It always helps to get an overview of the situation. Look for ladders.

- Rushing water turns the waterwheel.

- From the control tower, note the position of the big, wooden sluice gate. Where is it forcing water to go?

- Channel the water so it flows under the waterwheel.

The waterwheel still isn't turning, and that's the smoothest waterwheel I've ever seen.

- The flowing water needs something to push.

- Every waterwheel has flaps called "vanes" for the water to push, thus turning the wheel.

- Saavedro destroyed the mechanism that deploys this waterwheel's vanes. Find another way to deploy them.

- Explore the cylinder's interior.

- Deploy the vanes manually.

The waterwheel turns now, but it's not producing any electricity!

- Is the waterwheel gear linked to the turbine generator gear?

- Have you been out to the gear platform yet?

- The gears mesh under the gear platform.

- The big vertical gear on the waterwheel has to mesh with the big horizontal gear under the platform.

- The horizontal gear is too low.

I found the emergency gear release, but when I try to raise the gear, it won't go!

- You can't mesh two gears while one is turning.

- The waterwheel gear must be stationary before you can raise the generator gear.

- Stop the waterwheel, then try again.

- But if you just move the sluice gate to direct water away from the waterwheel, you can't get back down to the gear release room.

- You can't raise the gear unless water is flowing under the waterwheel without turning it. How can you do that?

Electromagnet Chamber

The power plant is running, and the door on the gear platform is open. Now I'm in a big chamber full of coils with a big cylinder surrounded by five platforms. What next?

- Examine the cylinder.

- Find an aperture and look through it. To borrow a line from Atrus' grandmother Anna, "What do you see?"

- Yes, you see circuits. Are all of the connector pins lined up?

- Align the connector pins.

Fig. 7-7. The pins at bottom are connected here, but the ones at top are not. You need connected circuits in all five aperture views.

- Push the side buttons to rotate the circuit strips until all circuits are connected. (Each of the three circuit strips runs completely around the inside of the cylinder.)

- You must create unbroken paths from each bottom connector pin to a top pin, and each top connector pin to a bottom pin.

- Align the top strip first, making sure all top pins are connected. Then align the bottom strip with the bottom pins. Finally, rotate the middle strip, looking for matches.

- If the circuit is complete in one aperture view but power still isn't flowing, check the other aperture views. The circuits must be properly aligned in *all five views*.

- Good luck!

The electromagnet is humming with power. Now what?

- You've done all you can do on this half of the island for now.

- Travel to an entirely new area.

- Head for the chasm.

- Backtrack through the power plant and tunnels.

Airship Dry Dock

I found the lever that opens the big, circular, segmented door. But it just closes back up!

- Doors generally open to let something in or out.

- Something can exit via the door, but it's not ready to go yet.

- Go around the door to see what's in the cavern behind it.

That's a cool-looking airship, but somebody trashed the access walkway. How can I reach it?

- You can't reach the airship from this dry dock area.

- Move the ship to the next place you can board.

- Move the ship to the chasm gantry tower.

How can I move the airship? It looks flat.

- Inflate the ship.

- Pump pressurized hot air from the dry dock's pressure valves into the ship.

But I tried the pressure valves. Nothing happens!

🦋 Is hot air flowing into the valve tower? You can't pressurize air that isn't flowing.

🦋 Direct hot air from the lava chamber into the dry dock valves.

Lava Chamber

What lava chamber? I can't find any lava chamber!

🦋 That's because Saavedro jammed its door (found back in the tunnels) from the inside. The only other way into the lava chamber is *very* roundabout.

🦋 That big, segmented pipe above the chasm is a hot air conduit. It feeds superheated air back to the dry dock valves. Do you suppose a lava chamber might be a good source of hot air? (What an insightful question!)

🦋 Look for out-of-the-way hatches and a precarious pathway across the chasm.

🦋 Search the valve tower area in the airship dry dock. Be thorough.

🦋 Find a maintenance hatch located high up.

🦋 Cross the chasm on the pipe and find another hatch.

🦋 In the long ventilation duct, look *thoroughly* for exits.

These lava chamber mechanisms are fun, but what am I trying to accomplish?

🦋 Blow hot air down the conduit to the dry dock.

🦋 What sort of device blows air?

🦋 Look through the window at the far wall of the lava containment room. See the fan up high?

🦋 Is the fan turning? (We'll help you here: No, it's not.) Look for the on/off switch near the fan.

🦋 Turn on the fan.

🦋 Your ultimate goal is to get lava flowing through the containment room while the fan is blowing. This sends hot air down the conduit to the dry dock valves.

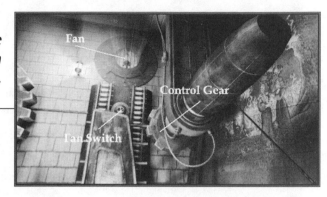

Fig. 7-8. Use the lava chamber controls to operate the control gear so you can reach the fan switch to turn on that fan.

How do I turn on the fan?

✦ Get inside the lava containment room and raise the catwalk to the fan switch.

✦ It's tricky, though. You can't enter the chamber until you empty out the lava.

✦ Note the vertical endplate on the catwalk. See the hole in it? It uncovers the fan switch when you raise the catwalk high enough.

How do the lava chamber controls work?

✦ First, note that the lava chamber has redundant controls: one podium up in the control room (in front of the window), one podium down on the catwalk in the containment room.

✦ However, the control room podium has been sabotaged; Saavedro jammed a bolt into it. You can't slide the red knob across the center groove.

✦ The red knob activates a "control gear" in the containment room. Attached to a moveable mechanical arm, this control gear opens/closes lava gates while at the same time moving the catwalk up/down. The inflow gate (left) lets lava in, and the drain gate (right) lets lava out.

✦ Rotate the red knob clockwise and watch what the control gear does in the containment room. Which way does it turn? Now try counterclockwise. Which way does the control gear turn?

✦ What happens to the catwalk when the control gear turns?

✦ After you drain out lava, enter the containment room and check out the control podium. Slide the red knob across the center groove and watch what happens.

✦ So by using the red knobs on the podiums, you must manipulate the control gear and complete the following tasks:

1. Empty the containment room of lava.
2. Raise the catwalk up to the fan switch.
3. Turn on the fan.

4. Lower the catwalk and return to the safety of the control room.
5. Make lava flow through the containment room—both lava gates up!

The Valve Puzzle

What do all these valves do?

- They pressurize the hot air flowing in from the lava chamber.

- If hot air isn't venting from the valve caps, you probably haven't solved the lava chamber puzzle yet. (See the previous section, "Lava Chamber.") Or else you closed the valves earlier, maybe while experimenting.

- Open valves (cap up) vent hot air, reducing pressure. Closed valves (cap down) channel hot air to the release valve, increasing pressure.

- When set to the correct pressure reading, the valves can pump hot air to the airship and inflate its balloon.

What's the correct pressure reading for inflating the airship?

- Check the pressure gauge.

- See the red line?

- Clockwise movement of the needle indicates pressure is increasing.

Do all the valves pump the same pressure? How many valves are there?

- Good questions. Both are easy enough to test.

- Close a valve on the first level and watch the gauge. How much pressure is added? Repeat for each valve.

- All valves (including the jammed one) on the first level produce the same amount of pressure.

- Ride the elevator to see how many other valves are in the tower.

Fig. 7-9. Pressure increases when valves are closed, like the two on the right; pressure decreases when valves are opened, like the two on the left.

The valve tower elevator doesn't move when I pull the handle.

- The elevator is pneumatic (powered by air pressure). Apparently, there's not enough pressure built up in the valve system.

- Close some valves to build pressure.

- The colors on the gauge show how much pressure is needed to push the elevator to each level.

I know how much pressure each tier puts out per valve, and how much pressure inflates the airship, but I keep having elevator problems.

- Keep closing valves, building elevator pressure and working your way up to the top tier of valves.

- Figure out the math. Because of the valve jammed in the closed position on the bottom tier, there's only one solution.

- Now work your way down, opening valves to get the units of pressure you want to produce from each tier.

- When you get the exact pressure indicated on the gauge's red line, find the big release valve.

I released the airship! But it got stuck at the dry dock door.

- Count to 1.3 million by ones.

- Try to grasp the concept of infinity. Keep thinking about it until you go insane.

- Do a bunch of other stuff.

- Go open the door!

- The lever that opens the dry dock door is on the chasm's gantry platform—a quick elevator ride down.

Back to J'nanin

I'm back with the symbol sketch in my inventory. Now what?

- The symbol itself triggers something in the room.

- Enter the symbol into the machine.

- Take the symbol from inventory and place it on the imaging table.

Hints for Amateria: Age of Dynamic Forces

Amateria features a twisting, looping network of tracks running through a series of odd structures arrayed around a huge central tower. Exploration reveals that each structure is connected to the tower by two sets of tracks: one set running out from the tower's roof, and another running into a lower section of the tower.

Arrival

This place is like a carnival, but none of the tracks are connected. What's the point?

Fig. 7-10. Tracks seem to run everywhere in Amateria. But none of the track circuits are completely connected.

- Many of Atrus' lessons involve completing a connection.

- Each of the major structures is part of a track circuit.

- But in each structure, the circuit is incomplete; an ice sphere shatters at some point in the circuit.

- Complete each track circuit.

Balance Bridge

No matter where I set the fulcrum under the half-pipe bridge, it still tilts up and smashes the ice sphere. How can I keep the bridge level?

- What tilts the bridge?

- Can you do something to offset the tilt?

- Create a counterbalance.

I found the balance connected to the other end of the bridge. How much weight should I put on it?

- How much weight are you trying to counterbalance?

- Go out and examine the multicolored sphere—the one that gets knocked into the bridge's catch-basket. What's it made of?

- Be sure to examine *both* sides of the multicolored sphere. You can find two good angles for close-up views.

- Compare the various sphere wedges near the counterbalance. Do you know the weight ratios between the various materials (wood, crystal, and metal)?

- You'll find the weight ratios in Saavedro's room back in J'nanin.

Saavedro smashed so many weights I can't create a one-to-one weight ratio with the sphere in the bridge catch-basket. How can I balance a weight I can't match?

- How did Saavedro do it?

- Look in Saavedro's room in the J'nanin Observatory for a clue.

- Saavedro figured out a way to balance a 2-to-1 weight ratio. Maybe you can do the same.

- Use a fulcrum.

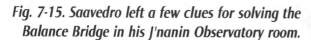

Fig. 7-15. Saavedro left a few clues for solving the Balance Bridge in his J'nanin Observatory room.

The Resonance Rings

The ice spheres keep smashing into these clear vibrating rings. How can I turn them all off?

- You can't turn them all off—not all at once, anyway.

- But you can set a mechanism to turn them off one at a time, in order, so that the ice sphere rolls through safely.

- The sonic barriers are generated by the blue crystals atop the nearby columns.

- Each crystal produces a harmonic frequency to form its ring. You can manually adjust the frequency to one of five settings.

- When pressed, each blue button on the Resonance Ring's main control panel turns off a particular frequency in the structure.

- Think about that. The crystals out on the Resonance Ring *generate* frequencies to create the barriers, but the control panel buttons *disable* frequencies.

- The control panel is actually a timing mechanism. Note how the ball bearing rolls over the five blue buttons in a timed sequence.

Other than by trial and error, how can I tell which frequency each button on the main control panel turns off?

- If this question makes no sense to you, better check out the preceding packets of hints.

- What common elements does the Resonance Ring main control panel share with the frequency dials on each crystal's column?

- The gear shape around the first console button indicates which frequency that button disables.

I understand how the gear shapes indicate which button turns off which frequency. But now what?

- Get out on the tracks and think like a ball.

- What path would a sphere take through the Resonance Ring loops if, say, the Resonance Rings were disabled, one by one, just before the sphere reached each ring?

- The first button in the control panel timing sequence should turn off the first Resonance Ring in the ice sphere's route from the Central Tower. The second button should turn off the second ring in the sphere's route, and so on.

🕊 So you must set the first Resonance Ring in the sphere's path to the same frequency turned off by the first button in the control panel sequence. Confused?

🕊 Walk the path of the rolling ice sphere, setting the frequency of each ring to match the order of the buttons on the control panel.

Turntable Tracks

What am I trying to do here?

🕊 Complete the circuit.

🕊 As at each Amateria structure, you're trying to guide an ice sphere through the track mechanism and back to the Central Tower.

🕊 Set the mechanism so the ice sphere drops through an open ring in the top-left hole of the right wheel. This puts the sphere on a return track to the tower.

What's the purpose of the dials on the control panel?

🕊 Pull the ball release lever. As the dial rotates, what else happens?

🕊 The dial rotation controls the wheel rotation out on the structure.

🕊 The left dial controls the left wheel, and the right dial controls the right wheel.

Fig. 7-12. Powerful springs in the wheel holes can shoot the ice spheres from wheel to wheel, but only if aligned with those track arches curving over the top of the structure.

Why does the ice sphere shatter sometimes?

🔹 The ice sphere shatters when it has no place to go.

🔹 The sphere drops and shatters if it lands in an open ring with no track underneath.

🔹 The "filled" rings on each wheel have a powerful spring mechanism that shoots the sphere when the wheel's rotation halts.

🔹 Note the four sets of curved track over the top of the Wheels of Wonder structure. Springs can shoot ice spheres across these tracks to the opposite wheel.

🔹 The sphere shatters if it lands in a spring-filled ring and then gets rotated to a position with no track arch to direct it to the opposite wheel.

What do I do with the pegs in the control panel's tray?

🔹 Plug in a peg on the left dial and see what happens. What happens to the dial? What happens to the peg?

🔹 Without a peg, the dial (and its corresponding wheel) makes one complete turn.

🔹 The peg controls the dial's rotation.

🔹 Set the pegs so that the ice sphere rotates to positions where the spring mechanism can shoot it over the track arches to the opposite wheel.

The Central Tower

The colored buttons above me release ice spheres from the tower, but they shatter when they return. Is that good or bad?

🔹 Shattering spheres generally indicate an incomplete circuit.

🔹 Look down. Looks like a big switchyard of unconnected tracks.

🔹 Your final task in Amateria is to link all of the individual track circuits into one grand, connected circuit.

What am I trying to do at this control panel?

🔹 Make connections, as always.

🔹 Actually, you're trying to make one big connection.

🔹 Rotate the track disks until you make an unbroken path.

🔹 Connect all four Amateria structures Resonance Rings, Balance Bridge, Turntable Tracks, and the offshore structure) into a single track circuit through the Central Tower switchyard.

Why?

- Your goal all along has been to reach the mysterious offshore structure, the one with the missing sections of track.

- What did you see on each control panel after you solved the puzzles at the Resonance Rings, Balance Bridge, and Turntable Tracks?

- If you can connect all three track circuits to the offshore structure, you can raise its three missing track sections.

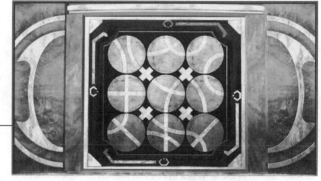

Fig. 7-13. Connect all of the Amateria track circuits into one big circuit with this switchyard control console.

I understand how to rotate console disks to connect the tracks in the switchyard below. But how do I know what structures I'm connecting on the console?

- Colors.

- In Amateria, structures are color-coded.

- Did you notice different color borders around the hexagon codes after you solved each Amateria puzzle?

- The ceiling buttons are color-coded, too. What happens when you push each one?

- Look at the console. See the color segments around the outside? Each represents one of the structures around Amateria.

Hints for Edanna: Age of Nature

Your ultimate goal in Edanna, as in the other Ages, is to find its unique symbol. To do so, you must first discover how various plants and animals in the Age react to different stimuli: light, touch, the presence of symbiotic and predatory plants and creatures, and so on. As you explore, remember the enlightened observation in Atrus' journal: "Nature encourages mutual dependence."

Deadwood Ridge

I climbed the first Corkscrew Cattail and saw the birds. But the other cattail is dry and shriveled. I'm stuck!

- Did you notice any difference between the two cattails? Look carefully at the entire plant.

- Each cattail has a drinking tendril. But one tendril found water, and one didn't.

- The dry cattail's tendril extends to a dry basin.

Fig. 7-14. Corkscrew Cattails need water to unfurl their convenient spiral leaves.

How can I hydrate the dry cattail?

- Touch that big swollen Quaffler Fig pod hanging over the dry basin. What's sloshing around inside?

- Pop the pod.

- Zap it with a beam of concentrated light. Got a laser handy? How about a magnifying glass?

- No? OK, explore the entire upper ridge area.

- Find an Aurora Blossom on a promontory and look through its lens. What do you see down below?

- Some sun can help the big flower get focused.

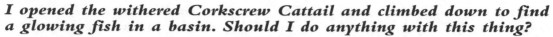

I opened the withered Corkscrew Cattail and climbed down to find a glowing fish in a basin. Should I do anything with this thing?

- Yes, but not here.

- Before you move on, watch the fish awhile. It's an Electra Ray. What happens when it feeds on the nearby plant roots?

- Note the thick, tube-like vine running from the bottom of the basin.

- Continue down the path. See how the tube-like vine from above sprouts a spiky fig pod?

- This is all part of another Quaffler Fig plant system. The vine and pods can draw water from the basin, which is actually the flowering top of the plant.

- Fig pods are sensitive to the touch.

Fig. 7-15. Move this Electra Ray down to Edanna's forest via a unique, 100-percent organic transport system.

The Bungee Swing Vine

How do I unroll this big, curled Tongue Fern?

- Tongue Ferns respond to light.

- Atrus designed this Age to exhibit the "mutual dependence" of species. Find something nearby that provides a stimuli to the fern.

- Use the symbiotic spore as a lantern.

The Tongue Fern doesn't reach anything!

- Actually, it does. But you have to look around.

- Walk to the tip of the fern and look up.

I can swing off the side of the Tongue Fern to the ledge with the trap. But the log-bridge blocks my swing in the other direction.

- You can knock the log down, but you'll need help from both flora and fauna.

- What grows on the log?

- Remember your previous experience with Barnacle Moss.

- If you can get the moss buds to expand, that rotting log might just break apart. What makes Barnacle Moss expand?

- A Squee lives nearby.

- Get the Squee over to the log.

How do I get the Squee out of its nest?

- The Squee built its nest here because one of its favorite foods is nearby. (No, not the Barnacle Moss.)

- Squees love pink fruit.

- Lure the Squee with a pink fruit.

I trap the Squee, but when I raise the trap, he just runs away.

- You don't want to trap the Squee.

- Note where the trap falls.

- The fallen trap blocks the entrance to the Squee's nest.

- Lure the Squee to a spot other then directly under the trap.

Edanna Forest

The poor mother bird is trapped in the Venus flytrap. Do I care? What can I do about it?

- Yes you care, if only for self-serving reasons. Ultimately, the mother Grossamery can do you a big favor, but not if she ends up as digested bird pulp.

- You need to open the plant's trap. But how?

- The Venus flytrap needs a good jolt.

Fig. 7-16. This little experiment back in J'nanin hints at how you can open Edanna's big Venus flytrap to release the mother bird.

🐦 Remember the smaller flytrap on Saavedro's work desk in the J'nanin Observatory?

🐦 Did you try hooking the smaller flytrap's roots to the battery? If so, what happened when you zapped them?

🐦 Zap the big flytrap's roots with electricity.

Where can I find electricity in Edanna? I haven't seen anything even remotely technological!

🐦 Find a natural source of electrical current.

🐦 Remember the fish's root feast up in the basin above the bungee swing vine area?

🐦 Move the Electra Ray down to the roots of the Venus flytrap.

How can I carry the fish? Won't it hurt?

🐦 You can't carry an Electra Ray. It hurts.

🐦 Use a natural delivery system.

🐦 One Quaffler Fig plant sprouts a number of pods, all connected by the same tube-like vine.

🐦 Didn't you already suck the water and fish down into the pod near the swing vine puzzle?

🐦 Keep an eye out for more fig pods.

I got the fish down to the pod hanging over the basin with the Venus flytrap roots. Now what?

🐦 Remember your pod-popping experience back up on Deadwood Ridge?

🐦 Find another Aurora Blossom—the big yellow flower with an amber focusing lens.

I see another Aurora Blossom across the forest, but the Tongue Fern leading to that side won't open; it doesn't have a symbiotic spore to shed light.

🐦 Find a different source of light.

🐦 Direct sunlight to the Tongue Fern.

🐦 See those orchid-like flowers hanging from vines around the edges of the forest? Those are Lambent Orchids, and they have interesting petals.

🐦 Set up a reflection system using the mirror-like petals of the orchids.

🐦 Start with the one orchid that sits in sunlight.

I found another Aurora Blossom. But it's not in the sunlight!

🐦 Direct sunlight to the Aurora Blossom.

🐦 Adjust your orchid reflection system to hit the blossom.

I popped the pod, and the Grossamery is free. What next?

🐦 Drop down into the swamp.

🐦 Find the bungee vine that lowers you to the swamp level.

🐦 To find the vine, explore the path you took from the Tongue Fern up to the Aurora Blossom.

🐦 Examine the area inside the open, hollow branch (the one lit by glowing mushrooms).

🐦 Near the top, where gaps in the trunk reveal the ocean outside, look for another branch that's frayed open and hollow, too.

Edanna Swamp

What's up with these two big white plants in the swamp?

🐦 Remember the succulent fruit you saw the mother Grossamery feeding her hatchling up in the nest?

🐦 The succulents come from the Nemel Lotus. The birds really, really love Nemel fruit.

🐦 The open lotus is picked clean of fruit, the closed lotus is untouched.

Why should I care what birds like to eat?

🐦 Remember the Lens Blossom view near your arrival in Edanna? You saw a book encased in a vine cage hanging directly beneath the bird's nest.

🐦 Could that be another J'nanin linking book?

🐦 If so, could it be near the Edanna Age symbol?

🐦 The only way to reach the vine tangle is via the nest.

🐦 The only way to reach the nest is via the bird.

🐦 If you find another stash of succulents, maybe you could hitch a ride up.

Fig. 7-17. What does this open Nemel Lotus have that the other, closed lotus doesn't?

How do I open up the closed Nemel Lotus?

🐦 Compare its status to the open lotus in the other chamber.

🐦 The open lotus sits in sunlight and is swarming with insects. The closed lotus sits in a dark chamber.

🐦 No direct sunlight enters the dark chamber of the closed Nemel Lotus. Find some indirect lighting.

🐦 Look for another Lambent Orchid in the dark chamber.

I got sunlight shining on the closed Nemel Lotus. But it still won't open up!

- Light only unfurls the twin stamens atop the plant.

- What else does the open Nemel Lotus have that the closed one doesn't?

- When a Nemel's stamen unfurls, it presents its pollen-producing anther, which attracts pollinating insects.

- A pollinating insect, being an incredibly intelligent entity, won't desert a good thing until it has to.

- You need to retract the stamen pair of the Nemel Lotus in the lighter chamber, thus hiding its pollen, or the pollinating insects will never leave.

- Remember what element makes the stamen of a Nemel Lotus unfurl? Eliminate that element in the open lotus' chamber.

OK, I took your advice and blocked the sunlight to the open Nemel Lotus. The stupid insects still won't leave!

- They just need a little incentive.

- They won't leave unless something chases them away.

- Find something nearby that insects despise.

- Insects hate spores from the Vesuvi Mushroom, a ball-shaped fungus that grows in swamps.

- The Vesuvi Mushroom erupts with spores when touched.

- But spores only travel so far. Find a Vesuvi Mushroom close enough to do the job.

Success! The other Nemel Lotus is open and ripe for the picking. Now what?

- Hop aboard the succulent express.

- Get inside the newly opened Nemel Lotus.

- Unfortunately, you can't climb directly into the pod. You have to find another way in.

- The Nemel Lotus root is purple, hollow, and very, very long.

- Find the plant's root.

I'm hanging in a wild fruit cage. But how can I lure the bird down here?

- The Grossamery responds to the popping sound of the fruit stem when it shoots seeds.

- Pull the stem and hang on tight.

Hints for Narayan: Age of Balance

I linked into a room that has two podiums and a switch that looks important. But nothing happens when I manipulate them.

- They need power.

- A generator that draws energy from geothermal vents powers this linking chamber.

- The switch that channels power from the generator to the devices is turned off.

- Find the power switch and turn it on.

I'm trapped in an ice shield with an angry guy with a hammer. How do I get out?

- Disable the ice shield.

- Find the shield activation controls and enter the code.

- Remember those devices downstairs?

I powered up the podium consoles, but now I'm looking at a bunch of circles—a code box, clearly. Where can I find the code?

- Check out the tapestries.

- Do any of the tapestry glyphs look familiar?

- Note that each glyph is associated with a word. Do any of the tapestry words look familiar?

The words associated with glyphs on the tapestries are generic terms, yet some of them seem familiar in a specific way. Where have I seen them before?

- If you've been thorough, you read them earlier in the game.

- Actually, you have the words at your disposal right now.

- Atrus gave you the words (*and* their correct order) a long time ago.

- Check your inventory.

Aha! Using the tapestries and Atrus' journal, I figured out which four glyphs form each symbol. But where does each glyph go?

- Look for clues in your inventory.

- Don't you have some partial symbols?

- Examine your symbol sketches.

- Compare the glyphs in the sketches to the mantras in Atrus' journal.

- Look at the symbol you found in Edanna. What's the first word in Atrus' Nature mantra? Where is that word's corresponding glyph (from the tapestries) positioned on the Age symbol?

I finally entered the correct glyphs on the console that controls the inner shield. But I can't find the tapestry glyphs for the other console.

- They're in another room.

- After you disabled the inner shield to the glide ship, did you explore?

I found the Tomahna linking book! Should I leave now before Saavedro gets hammer happy?

- When you have the Tomahna book, you can leave anytime you want. But carefully consider the situation and the possible consequences.

- Have you retrieved the Releeshahn book yet?

- What was the last thing Saavedro told you when you met him upstairs?

- Didn't it sound kind of ominous when Saavedro pointed out that "the one thing I know about linking books— the doors they open don't close behind you"?

Saavedro wants me to open the outer shield. In return, he promises to give me the Releeshahn book for Atrus. Should I trust him? Or should I go out to the glide ship and confront him?

Fig. 7-18. Should you trust this man?

- Saavedro wandered in a fog of insanity for 20 years, exiled to a strange land and separated from his family, who he now presumes is dead. And he blames Atrus for his excruciating set of personal circumstances. Think about it.

- Saavedro is very angry, and he's been waving around a pretty ugly-looking hammer.

- Try a third option.

- At this point, you should get Saavedro in a situation where he's under your control.

- Trap Saavedro between the shields.

- Remember how the shields were deployed when you first arrived? What's the first thing you did in your attempt to change it?

I trapped Saavedro and he gave me the book. Can I go now?

- Sure.

- After all, Saavedro hasn't suffered enough yet. Twenty years is nothing, really.

- Think how much fun it would be to leave this tormented fellow stranded with the knowledge that his civilization (and perhaps family) thrives just out of reach, across the ice barrier. It might be interesting, in a clinical sort of way, to see how he reacts.

- You heartless cad.

Chapter 8
Historian's Journal
On the Narayan Exile and the Lesson Age of Atrus

Warning! Do not read the following chapter until you have finished the game!

Note: This historical record of developments leading up to the events of *Myst III: Exile* reveals central story elements of the game. Reading it before finishing the game may reduce significantly the dramatic impact of the story.

Evidence culled from Atrus' personal journals and other contemporary records attest to the Master's desire to teach sons Sirrus and Achenar the D'ni craft of writing Ages ("The Art"). However, knowing how poorly his own father Gehn had taught him—and taking a cue from his grandmother, Anna, who continually asked him to "tell [me] what you see"—Atrus believed the first steps in the boys' education should be observational. So, he designed a course of study that would encourage his sons to closely observe, in action, the most fundamental principles shared by all stable Ages. (Ed. note: Ironically, neither son learned to write.) To this end, Atrus authored what he termed his Lesson Age.

Atrus Creates the Lesson Age

Carefully crafted to provide an experiential demonstration of Age-building concepts, the Lesson Age provides a classic example of the "cluster design" philosophy favored by Atrus and certain other D'ni Masters of the ancient art. In standard fashion, Atrus first created a hub world, J'nanin, often referred to as "the Lesson Age." This island Age functions as a kind of primer and as a central link to four separate Element Ages (three uninhabited), each of which embodies one important principle.

All three of the uninhabited Element Ages—Voltaic (Energy), Amateria (Dynamic Force), and Edanna (Nature)—were crafted to be studied, understood, and "solved" in order to unlock the book to the Fourth Age, Narayan, a living civilization based on a delicate symbiosis of elements. Indeed, Narayan (according to the Master's design notes) was conceived as a culmination of all learning, teaching Atrus's fourth and central principle: Balance of various systems can enable a civilization to thrive.

Atrus devised the following process for his students: Learn the three primary principles of Age-building through a course of direct observation and interaction with the first three Ages. At the end of the studies on each Age, uncover a symbol that upon discovery has no obvious inherent meaning. Students return to the J'nanin hub world with each symbol and enter it into a mechanism; each symbol triggers a hologram recording from Atrus explaining in detail the lessons realized from the observation of each age. (Ed. Note: Unfortunately, archivists have been unable to restore these lesson recordings, which were recorded over and thus erased by Saavedro. More on this below.)

When students enter the third symbol (apparently, the order of entry is unimportant), the mechanism holding the Narayani book unlocks. This book provides access to a curiously sealed linking chamber in the Age of Balance, where a final test is administered: Students must use an array of Narayan tapestries to translate the three Age symbols and discover that each symbol summarizes a basic concept of Age-writing. In the particular case of Sirrus and Achenar, it is assumed by scholars who've studied the record that the boys would recognize these concepts because, according to journal evidence and records of personal correspondence, Atrus had been discussing them with his sons for years.

Atrus formally recorded these first three concepts in his Journal of Releeshahn:

- Energy powers future motion.

- Nature encourages mutual dependence.

- Dynamic forces spur change.

Atrus expected that through deductive reasoning his sons would realize that the important fourth concept was not yet represented: "Balanced systems stimulate civilization." Presumably, they would then create it themselves, using Narayani tapestries to disable the crystal-generated ice shield sealing the linking chamber. Upon gaining access to Narayan, Sirrus and Achenar could enter and meet a specially appointed tutor, Saavedro, to guide them through the experience of the final concept.

The last step of Atrus's course required students to live on Narayan and see how its civilization was the living embodiment of the Balance concept. In his own journal, Saavedro writes how Atrus spoke of this final step in his sons' education: "Narayan is the sum of what they must learn."

Narayan's Symbiosis: Culture and Tradition

Narayan is a water world. Civilization indeed flourished in this Age, in accordance with the well-crafted descriptive book authored during one of Atrus's most prolific periods of Age-building. Yet human existence in this Age is based on a precarious, carefully managed symbiotic relationship between two life forms.

The first, a large, algae-like plant that the Narayanis call "lattice," grows in abundance around underwater geothermal vents, where the heated water produces copious mineral sediment. Well-nourished lattice roots are thick, nearly impenetrable, and can extend great lengths—some nearly a mile long—with numerous tendrils and branches forming a weblike latticework from the central stalk or stem.

The second life form, huge airborne spore sacs known as "puffer spores," abound in the Narayan atmosphere. These spores periodically migrate to the underwater geothermal vents to replenish themselves with the hot carbon gases emitted there. After this migration, a reinflated spore typically floats up to the ocean surface and reenters the atmosphere. There, its respiration (a simple molecular gas exchange) slowly releases oxygen to replenish the Narayan atmosphere.

Narayani civilization (as scripted by Master Atrus) is entirely founded upon its ability to capture puffer spores drifting from the geothermal vents, use them to support growing lattice so that the roots grow upward, and thereby form "Lattice Trees," the foundation on which Narayani cities exist. To create stable lattice-based structures, Narayanis must hand-weave the roots into netlike enclosures around the airborne spores.

As one might expect, these lattice-root structures constantly must be maintained. Narayani guide manuals of the time point out that "if the lattice is not trimmed constantly, the root-net eventually will smother the spores. But if roots are over trimmed, the spores may break free, destroying the delicate balance between the two." Over time, this maintenance process developed into ritualistic traditions. Indeed, it has been estimated that, according to the dictates of survival, as much as 80 percent of waking hours on Narayan was devoted to highly structured activities that tend to the Age's ecosystem.

Thus it can be said that Narayani civilization is quite tradition-bound, built upon a fairly rigorous discipline in the form of ceremonies that, by necessity, serve the purpose of maintaining the Age's lattice-root infrastructure.

Atrus and Saavedro

Recently recovered journal evidence has documented Atrus's first visit to Narayan, where he met and befriended Saavedro, a young scholar and teacher highly regarded in that Age. Atrus asked Saavedro to be guardian and guide for his sons—in particular, to teach them Narayan's unique culture based on symbiotic balance.

Here is an excerpt from Saavedro's personal journal describing not only the lattice-weave and spore-capture processes, but also the nature of the relationship between the two men:

This Atrus stayed with us for months. I taught him how to trim the delicate lattice roots. How to splice old and new growths together so the walls of our houses will grow strong. I tell him the traditions of the

Weave. How, by using the spores to support the growing branches, we keep the Lattice Tree alive. He wants to learn everything I know. He wants Narayan to survive.

I take him to the rift, to where the sea flows through gaps in the world. Steam flows up from the waterfall. The puffer spores are ready to take flight. We stand in the shadows of dusk and watch the spores begin to rise. He says they look like pearls against the sky. Then he points to one of the spores. It's smaller than the rest. Small enough to fit the niche we'd woven into the branches that morning. Its skin is milky white. With just the faintest touch of pink.

That one, Atrus said. That should support your new daughter's room perfectly, I think.

I remember I nodded. Then I raised my pipe and played. Atrus stood beside me, holding his breath as my song drew the hollow spore in close. As soon as it was near he threw the net and dragged it in.

This is what I remember.

This is why I said he could send me his sons.

However, later records indicate that Sirrus and Achenar, despite passing the Lesson Age course with alacrity, did not respond well to their stay in Narayan. Saavedro himself wrote that although they resembled their father in physical ways, "they are different somehow, too. They're more impatient. And they are angry not to be treated like men." Interview transcripts of the period refer to their obvious boredom and, according to one eyewitness claim, "thinly veiled insolence." Surviving hologram recordings even speak of "two very greedy little boys." Yet, according to contemporary accounts, Atrus suspected none of this upon his return to escort the boys home.

Unfortunately for Narayani society, Sirrus and Achenar returned as young men approximately five years later. This visit occurred just prior to their well-documented Myst Island period, during which they conspired to plunder and subjugate Ages stored in the Myst library to seek power and wealth. In essence, Narayan became the template for later crimes, including the subsequent rebellion against their father's authority. They considered the delicate Age "easy pickings" (as they would admit to Saavedro later in J'nanin), ripe for the disruption that could cover their larcenous activities.

Sirrus and Achenar: Decay of Narayan Tradition

It was the very fragility of the balance between man and nature that Sirrus and Achenar chose to exploit upon their return to Narayan. Narayani society had already begun to experience small fissures of inter-generational strain. In general, Narayani Elders—who understood the underlying significance of ceremonial traditions, having survived minor disasters due to faulty Lattice Tree maintenance—demanded strict adherence to the "Way of the Tree." But factions of younger Narayanis had begun to call into question the time-consuming rigor of these ceremonies.

Sirrus and Achenar, according to all accounts, were clever enough to recognize and exploit this burgeoning rift. For example, they tempted some of the more radical Narayani youth factions with claims of access to other Ages— alternative worlds, ready for emigration, where life was less rigorous. To manipulate those with no desire to leave Narayan, the brothers claimed to have their father's power (a lie), promising to fix Narayan's "fragility" by writing changes into the world. But this they would do only if *all* inhabitants concurred with such a course of action—knowing, of course, the Elders would never allow it.

In this manner, Sirrus and Achenar played Narayani society against itself. In the course of doing so, the brothers systematically undermined the authority of their own father, Atrus. Some contemporary documents report speeches railing against "the Creator" with such claims as this, attributed to Sirrus: "He wrote this Age, forcing you into an existence of insufferable toil…just to teach *us* lessons! Is that fair to you?"

With time, small insurrections (fomented by such talk) led to larger-scale riots and, eventually, an outbreak of civil war. The clash disrupted maintenance duties; within days, latticework structures began to degrade. As Saavedro writes in his journal:

> *The Lattice Roots were black from too much overgrowth. Puffer Spores floated up in the hot steam and burst. No one was there to guide the spores to the branches. No one was waiting to perform the ritual Weaves. The fighting had torn my people apart.*

Saavedro's Dilemma

Saavedro, it appears, was caught in the middle of the conflict in several ways. As the "good ambassador" between Atrus and Narayan, he had helped introduce Sirrus and Achenar to his society. Also, though not yet an Elder, he certainly hoped to earn that distinction. Yet Saavedro was more of a freethinker than many of the Elders (one document refers to him as a "dreamer-teacher"), so he was not an isolationist nor strictly tradition-bound. In fact, he may have found the brothers' claims credible at first. Story murals of the time depict him (often with his family) standing apart from the conflict—distressed, perhaps, but seemingly neutral, or even hopeful.

Meanwhile, Sirrus and Achenar stepped up their role as agitators, sowing discontent among the young, and encouraging civil unrest and violent resistance. But the brothers appear to have miscalculated how badly the chaos and disruption could endanger Narayan's physical existence; Lattice Tree failures decimated several villages. After a particularly nasty riot nearly led to their arrest by Elder loyalists, Sirrus and Achenar left Narayan for good.

Saavedro, apparently stunned by this sudden abandonment, found their linking book and followed them to J'nanin, hoping to convince them to carry out their promises and save Narayan. But the brothers captured Saavedro. According to his own account, they beat him severely, tied him to one of the reflection poles in J'nanin, built a bonfire in front of him, and linked back to Myst over the fire, thus burning the linking book as the last brother disappeared. (Saavedro has described the agony of watching helplessly as his only chance of escape burns up in his face.)

Thus, Saavedo was trapped on J'nanin.

Saavedro on J'nanin

Being an educator and scholar himself, Saavedro soon grasped the nature of J'nanin. He spent several desperate months taking Atrus's Lesson Age course, learning the Age-building principles and solving the puzzles to unlock the Narayan book, all the while fearing that his family and people were dying.

When at last Saavedro linked to Narayan, he of course arrived inside the sealed linking chamber. Unlike Sirrus and Achenar, however, he was unable to decipher the final code that dissipates the outer ice shield. (Ed. Note: Sirrus and Achenar, having been raised by Atrus, knew the fourth, missing concept because their father constantly spoke of all four concepts during trips to other Ages.)

Upon arrival, Saavedro feared the worst. The ice shield's translucence gave but a distorted view of his world. Torn Lattice Tree fragments, adrift in the atmosphere, suggested total devastation. In despair, Saavedro returned to J'nanin and fell into what his journal describes as "the fog": twenty tragic years of madness, punctuated by brief bouts of clarity and underlined by an ever-growing hatred for Atrus and his rapacious sons.

A New Link to J'nanin

During these two decades, the well-known events of Myst and Riven occurred. After the plunder and destruction of the Myst library by Sirrus and Achenar and their subsequent imprisonment, and following the cataclysmic final events on Riven, Atrus and his wife Catherine sought to revitalize D'ni civilization which had been decimated 75 years previously by a biological attack. The two spent many years searching the D'ni cavern and lost Ages, looking for those who might have survived the plague by virtue of escape and resettlement. These events are carefully chronicled in *Myst: The Book of D'ni* (Hyperion, 1997).

Atrus and Catherine eventually made contact with more than 1,800 D'ni survivors, many of whom joined their efforts to rebuild. But in the process Atrus came to realize that too much tragic history lay buried in the great city's ruins. He writes:

> *It should stand forever in ruins, as both a symbol of our past mistakes and a memorial to all who lost their lives when D'ni fell. If we rebuild the city walls today, are we not giving approval to the very illness that destroyed our civilization in the first place?*

And thus Atrus chose to write an entirely new world, named Releeshahn, for his D'ni people. (See Atrus's Journal of Releeshahn for more details.) Preparing for this task, he revisited many of his other Ages, looking for inspiration, reviewing concepts that had proved successful in the past. Again, according to a journal entry dated 93.10.28, just as he prepared to write this new Age, Catherine handed him "one of my oldest Age books." To this he adds:

> *Seeing the name "J'nanin" emblazoned on the Book cover, I could only shake my head. The one Age I never got around to revisiting was the one that might have helped me the most! I think, after I have finished this work, I should take one final trip——if only to help restore an old fool's memories!*

As soon as Atrus finished Releeshahn, he and Catherine built a new home for themselves, which they called Tomahna. And, as presaged in the journal entry, Atrus eventually did go to J'nanin. Subsequent records verify that he stayed only a short while, as memories of his sons and failures were too painful. Unbeknownst to Atrus, however, a witness lay in the high grass near the link arrival.

And when Atrus linked away, he left a Tomahna linking book behind—an escape route for Saavedro after more than twenty years of exile.

Saavedro's Scheme

By all accounts, Saavedro first linked into Tomahna with the express purpose of killing Atrus and his family. But Atrus and Catherine were gone, so he spent many hours poring over Atrus's journals, hoping to learn where Atrus, Catherine, and most importantly, the two sons were. (Ed. note: By this time, both Sirrus and Achenar had been banished to prison books in the Myst library.) In the course of this initial exploration, Saavedro made two significant discoveries.

First, he found Atrus's linking book to J'nanin tucked away in a study bookshelf. This gave him a route back to the Age of his exile. Second, he learned of Atrus's efforts to restore D'ni civilization. Misreading the Journal of Releeshahn text, Saavedro mistakenly assumed Atrus had the godlike ability to rewrite Ages, restore lost worlds, and repair disasters. This error probably saved Atrus's life, as Saavedro subsequently changed his focus from bloody revenge to a "kidnapping" plot. His new plan: Steal the Releeshahn descriptive book and hold it hostage in return for Atrus's restoration of Narayan civilization.

Back in J'nanin, Saavedro spent many months tampering with the lesson devices, altering the course and inserting hologram and imager messages (wiping out Atrus's own recordings) to reveal the story of his home world and the havoc wreaked there by Atrus's sons. He also painted three murals, one in each Age, depicting the events that transpired on Narayan. Finally, he scattered various pages of his journal around the Ages, knowing Atrus would eventually find them, too.

Then he set his plan in motion.

Little did Saavedro realize that not Atrus, but instead Atrus's most capable ally, would assume the challenge of tracking down the exile, reclaim Releeshahn, unlock the secrets of the past, and (as before in Myst and Riven) set right old wrongs.

Atrus' Journal

93.5.25

I always feared this day would come. For years, Catherine and I have dreamed of restoring D'ni. We have dedicated our lives to the task, taking it upon ourselves to locate the citizens of D'ni and convince them to return to their ruined city and rebuild. Our dream has become the dream of so many now, and the progress we have made toward achieving it is something of which we all can stand proud. But I know now that it has been a mistake.

The city of D'ni should not be restored. It should stand forever in ruins, as both a symbol of our past mistakes and a memorial to all who lost their lives when D'ni fell. The devastating events of recent months—the war on Terahnee, and the death of Uta, in particular—have driven this truth home to me quite forcefully. If we rebuild the city walls today, are we not giving approval to the very illness that destroyed our civilization in the first place? Are we not setting ourselves up to repeat that pattern again in future generations?

I have put much thought into this tonight and have found only one solution. If we, the men and women who survived the downfall of D'ni, are to thrive, then we must break the pattern of hatred which has destroyed so many lives. We must begin our civilization anew.

And we can only do that if I write us a new Age.

I have spoken with Catherine about this and she agrees. I only hope the others will see it, as well.

93.5.26

Will these people never cease to amaze me? I thought they would object to my decision. After all, most of them linked back to D'ni specifically to see the city rebuilt. But when I told them why we should not restore it, their response was immediate and unanimous. Whereas yesterday they thought only of rebuilding, today they concentrate solely on salvage. They intend to take from their ruined city only that which is best and move on.

Everywhere I look, the enthusiasm for this new task is obvious. It heartens me, even as I face my own monumental contribution. I have written many Ages in my lifetime—from my first timid attempts under the tyrannical tutelage of my father, to my most recent accomplishment, Averone. Never before has so much been riding on my skill. The Age I am about to write must be all I ever imagined and more. How am I going to achieve it?

93.6.1

Catherine laughed this morning when she saw me drudging out my old notebooks. I must have made quite the picture: sitting near the embers of a fire, surrounded by countless

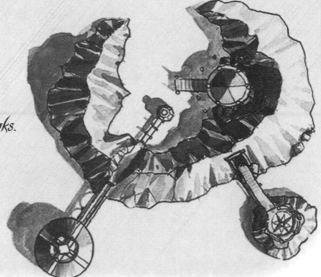

commentaries and journals. Some of them seemed more dust than paper. But the hours I spent sifting through them was worth it. Ideas for what this new Age might be are tumbling around in my head. There are almost too many to catch hold of.

Obviously, I must choose some starting point as my anchor. Writing Ages is a science—a precisely structured equation of words. Every equation needs as its foundation an underlying concept around which the Age can develop. In the past, I have written my Books around whatever idea intrigued me most at the time. I wanted to discover how the Age to which the Book linked would manifest the results of that idea. Sometimes civilizations had arisen. Sometimes they had not. But whether a society had come to exist on the Age or not, it was often in response to whatever concept the Book I had written embodied.

This time, my search for a concept must be weighed very carefully. I already have the civilization I wish to see develop. I know our history as a people, and the paths we have followed to arrive here. Today I must write a Book which will link to an Age that will allow us to continue on our way, growing ever stronger as one people. What underlying concept must this new Age reflect that will best allow our civilization to thrive?

I fear I must think on this some more.

93.6.5

It has taken me some time, but I may have found my anchor. It came to me as I was considering what I know about the survivors of D'ni. We have seen so much tragedy in our lives, from the destruction of the city, to the suffering and loss of loved ones due to plague and deprivation. Yet even in the midst of these adversities, my kinsmen and I have found the strength to keep going. We have tapped into our individual strengths and transformed ourselves into something much stronger.

It is a characteristic I have seen in several of my Ages, whenever I focused my Writing on the inherent energy sources in a world. Long ago, Grandmother taught me that no life—no possibility for life in an Age—exists without the presence of energy. By tapping into its latent energy sources, an Age moves out of stasis. It grows, transforms, and develops. Energy is the underlying fuel that powers all activity.

To put it more simply: <u>energy powers future motion.</u>

Yet, as Grandmother also liked to remind me, energy in an Age takes on diverse forms. Each one has strengths and weaknesses of its own. How many forms will this new Age contain? Which type will be its dominant theme?

Tomorrow I will link back to Myst, and from there revisit several of my Ages. Perhaps in my old worlds, I will discover new ideas.

93.6.6

I had almost forgotten how painful it is to revisit Myst. In the ten years since my sons, Sirrus and Achenar, left me trapped on K'veer Island and burned so many of my Books, Catherine and I have rarely linked back. I told myself we were always too busy. First with writing Ages like Averone, then with searching the Ages of D'ni for survivors. I always said we would spend more time on Myst eventually.

The truth is, I have been avoiding the Age. Seeing the island in its current condition ignites such anger and grief. I am immediately reminded of the betrayal of my sons, as well as the cruelty and greed with which they plundered my Ages. I know I am partly responsible for these acts. I constantly wonder if there were something I could have done to reach out to the boys before

Enough! Nothing can change the tragedies of the past. Like my D'ni kinsmen, I must salvage what is best and move on. Perhaps in the process, I will find forgiveness and hope.

93.10.17

Once again I am back on Myst island, having completed a lengthy sojourn through several of my Ages. The trip itself was not as inspiring as I had hoped. The Selenitic Age was especially disturbing–but has it not always been so? The very first time I linked to the Age, its uninhabited landscape was shaking with tremors. At the time, I felt it was because the energy in the Age was unfocused, as if it were at war with itself. Stability finally came but even after it did, I never truly felt comfortable there. I missed the more natural balance of Ages like Channelwood.

Perhaps that is the lesson to take home with me. The D'ni, too, have faced much turmoil in their history. Their lives have been unsettled enough. Perhaps I should be striving to offset the energy that already exists within our civilization by providing it with a more stabilized environment in which to grow. An environment in which the natural equilibrium of the world serves as a counterpoint to the upheavals of civilization.

The more I consider it, the more I wonder if I should make Nature the foundation of this new Age. Worlds like Channelwood attain equilibrium quite easily, primarily because of one reason: <u>nature encourages mutual dependence.</u> As one life withers and dies, it provides nourishment so that another might live. Plants become food for other animals, and the waste products animals cannot absorb become nutrients to sustain the other plants. So long as nothing intrudes to upset this balance, nature can maintain itself indefinitely.

An interesting metaphor to set as an example for my people!

I think I will confer with Catherine on this subject. Her Ages always exhibit symbiosis more dramatically than mine. Perhaps she should help me Write this new Age.

93.10.24

I am so tired, I can barely think right now. But I will force myself to stay focused, for I have not written anything in days. The moment I linked back to D'ni, I was besieged with requests for my assistance. Master Tamon wanted to consult over which stone cutters were worth salvaging - and did I think the rock in this new Age would be difficult to sound? Oma and Esel needed my opinion about a new history they had uncovered - should they hold off on starting its translation, or would paper supplies be scarce in the new Age? There were so many questions needing answers, I barely had time to see Catherine!

She, of course, laughed at my dilemma, saying that I had no one to blame but myself. After all, I was the one who encouraged the D'ni to start over. Naturally, they would look to me to keep them moving in the right direction, unless some other force stepped in to change that view.

Her words made me realize a fundamental principle I had thus far been ignoring. All this time, I have been debating whether to make energy or nature the underlying framework for this Age. But there is another equation to consider! An Age based solely on the future motion of energy will face constant upheavals, most likely at the cost of tranquility. And an Age based solely on the mutual dependence of nature can become so balanced over time, it may cease to tolerate change. Yet to continue to grow as a people, D'ni civilization needs both: occasional upheavals followed by periods of balanced stability.

I have seen such situations occur naturally on several of my Ages. Each time, it was because I centered the Writing around some dynamic force that I had decided to make prevalent in the Age. Such forces allow the balance between forward motion and mutual dependence to fluctuate. As one concept takes precedence, the other recedes until another force surfaces to change things. As Catherine's insightful comment reminded me, dynamic forces spur change.

I am too tired to think more on this tonight. Hopefully in the morning, my thoughts will coalesce.

93.10.25

Catherine surprised me today. Apparently while I was off visiting my
Ages, she linked to Myst by herself. She did not say so, but I could
tell that her visit had been painful. More than ever now, I am
convinced we must find a place to begin again ourselves.

Perhaps when I have written this new Age for the D'ni, I will put
some thought into where Catherine and I might live.

93.10.28

I cannot believe I did not I see it before! All this time I have been
struggling to describe the perfect Age for the D'ni. I have considered
and then rejected several underlying concepts which I felt might best set
the course for their future-as if I alone should determine how D'ni
civilization will grow! In my own way, I have become as egotistical as
my father!

In truth, I owe this realization to Catherine. Sensing my indecision
about the new Age, she led me on a walk around D'ni. Salvaging efforts
were well underway, with teams of people scouring the ruined harbor
district. As I watched my D'ni kinsmen deciding which parts of their
culture to retain, I realized they do not need me to determine their
future. They are quite capable of setting its course by themselves,
regardless of what Age I write!

This realization has opened my eyes to the best way of approaching my task. I no longer need to worry about which underlying concept—energy, nature, or dynamic forces—I should make prevalent in the Age. Rather, I must strive to include them all. I must write a balance of systems into the descriptive Book, enough so that the D'ni people will constantly be challenged to attain their ultimate potential. As Grandmother often pointed out to me when we spoke about Ages back on Myst, balanced systems stimulate civilizations.

At last I feel I am ready to begin Writing this Age. Indeed, I am eager to begin, and have already come up with the perfect name. I know Grandmother would have loved it!

Of course, Catherine could tell the moment I turned to her that I had finally found my starting point. I babbled on excitedly for some time before I noticed the smile she was hiding. When I saw it enough to grow suspicious, she handed me one of my oldest Age Books. She must have picked it up when she linked back to Myst. Seeing the name "J'nanin" emblazoned on the Book cover, I could only shake my head. The one Age I never got around to revisiting was the one that might have helped me the most! How foolish was I to have completely forgotten it.

I think, after I have finished this work, I should take one final trip—if only to help restore an old fool's memories!